TSQ Transgender Studies Quarterly

Volume 10 ∗ Number 2 ∗ May 2023

The Sports Issue

Edited by CJ Jones and Travers

T0021802

BOOK REVIEWS

The Sports Issue

An Introduction

CJ JONES and TRAVERS

Issues related to transgender participation have become highly visible items on the agendas of many sporting organizations, US legislatures, interscholastic organizations, and recreational leagues. Trans misogynist fascist movements are digging in, and right-wing conservatives are stoking fear around the specter of trans girls and women driving cisgender girls and women out of sport as a dog whistle to mobilize their base (Butler 2021). Coming on the heels of the US bathroom bills of the mid-2010s, anti-trans policies that target trans girls and women in the sociocultural realm of sports seem to deliver what the bathroom controversy only promised: urgent policing and surveillance of gender-suspicious bodies—down to the last molecule of testosterone—in rigidly gendered spaces. In the United States at the time of this writing, eighteen laws banning trans athletes from participating on teams that align with their gender identities have passed. In the 2022 legislative session alone, at least sixty-four bills were introduced in twenty-eight state legislatures, with names such as the Fairness in Women's Sports Act, Protect Women's Sports, and simply Biological Sex. Many of these laws erase transgender people entirely (Sharrow 2021) by defining sex simplistically as "biological sex at birth in accordance with the student's genetics and reproductive biology."[1] As Michelle Wolff, David A. Rubin, and Amanda Lock Swarr (2022: 151) observed in *TSQ*'s "Intersex Issue," "it is bitterly ironic that any legislation that mandates genital inspection for kids extends the biopolitical medicalization and regulation of intersex and trans* bodyminds to cis youth populations as well."

The assumption of biological advantage for male athletes is a central institutional feature of modern sports via sex-segregated sport or sex-differentiated activities within the same sport. For this reason, concerns about transgender participation in sport tend to crystallize around assumptions that transgender

TSQ: Transgender Studies Quarterly * Volume 10, Number 2 * May 2023
DOI 10.1215/23289252-10440734 © 2023 Duke University Press

women have an "unfair advantage" over cisgender women because of past exposure to "male" levels of testosterone (Cavanagh and Sykes 2006; Gleaves and Lehrbach 2016). The participation of trans boys and men is less controversial because of the presumed deficiencies of athletes who are assigned female at birth.

As today's sporting environments are an outgrowth of the precedents established when modern sport emerged in Europe and its colonies in the late nineteenth and early twentieth centuries as a capitalist, white supremacist, and heteropatriarchal "civilizing" project (Carter 2008; Carrington and McDonald 2009; Collins 2013), it is no accident that organized sport is a site for contesting the inclusion of transgender people and that these campaigns primarily target transgender girls and women for surveillance and exclusion. Binary sex differentiation and male superiority were central to the European ideology of "civilization," in contrast to "primitive" gender systems that were more fluid and egalitarian. This distinction between civilized and primitive was one of the key "moral" justifications for European colonialism and genocide. Modern sport was designed, through the deliberate exclusion of girls and women, to emphasize sex difference and to socialize boys and men into orthodox hetero-masculinity (Hargreaves 2013; Pronger 1990). The ideology of naturally occurring binary sex difference (Dreger 2000; Fausto-Sterling 2020; Fine 2017) is central to and integrated within a Eurocentric, white supremacist, colonial, and heteropatriarchal assemblage of power (Collins 2013; Higginbotham 1992; Puar 2007; Weheliye 2014; Wynter 2003). We cannot understand the experiences of trans athletes and policy debates about the terms of inclusion without seeing sport as part of this assemblage. Indeed, sport has a central role in naturalizing hierarchies of bodies and producing gendered and racialized norms (Douglas 2005, 2012; Pape 2017). Attacks on trans girls and women are consistent with modern sport's long-standing practice of policing female eligibility according to white, heteropatriarchal norms (Pieper 2016; Travers 2022).

Since *TSQ*'s publication of "Trans/Feminisms" in 2016, propelled in part by yet another book published by a well-established anti-trans, feminist academic, feminist anti-trans backlash both within and outside of the academy continue unabated (Stryker and Bettcher 2016). What interests us here is the relationship between anti-transgender positions and trans athleticism or, perhaps more specifically, the trenchant opposition to trans athletes' playing in a gendered sport (and sports team) that (best) aligns with their identity. In addition to organized anti-trans feminist groups that list sports as one item on their agenda, other groups have formed to make sport *the* feminist issue. For example, Save Women's Sports (n.d.), formed by amateur powerlifter Beth Stelzer in 2019, "seeks to preserve biology-based eligibility standards for participation in female sports. Fair Play for Women (n.d.), founded in the United Kingdom in 2018, is a campaigning and consultancy group whose efforts led World Rugby, the international governing body for the sport of rugby, to adopt a policy that allows only women assigned female at birth and women who transitioned prepuberty to compete in the women's division at the international level.[2] As Abraham Weil noted in a draft of our call for papers, these anti-trans feminist groups poke at the unfinished work of thinking about sex as a social construction. What makes sport so politically saturated in this context is that it is conveyed through the body, and the body, the myth goes, reveals the essence of a human being.

One of the questions that drove us to propose this special issue is why the realm of sports is a salient location wherein trans misogyny has gained political, discursive, and affective traction across the political spectrum. What are the conditions that enable so-called gender critical feminists,[3] anti-trans lawmakers, and various constituencies on the political right, as well as organizations and associations concerned with gender equity in sport, to conceive of various forms of harm against trans people as legitimate in response to issues including but not limited to sports, such as access to affirming health care, affordable housing, and employment protection? Drawing on tropes of the trans person as deceiver, cheater, suspect, and threat to cisgender women and girls, anti-trans social movements are pushing back against the gains trans social movements have achieved regarding inclusion in public life in the last few decades, with the ultimate goal of systemically eliminating us from public life. As Jules Gill-Peterson (2021) documents so powerfully, the full-scale erasure of transgender identities and people is part of a larger project that has been decades in the making.

A Trans Feminist Sport Studies Approach

Following Emi Koyama (2003), Marquis Bey (2022), and Finn Enke (2012), we understand trans feminism as an epistemological formation that does not simply view feminism through a transgender lens or add transness to feminism. Rather, trans feminism "is an assault on the genre of the [hierarchized] binary, that ontological caste that universalizes itself and structures how we are made possible" (Bey 2022: 53). Within the continuing scholarly and activist work loosely organized under the rubric of trans feminism, we want to explicitly interpolate a subfield called trans feminist sports studies (Jones 2021). Trans feminist sports studies seeks to unravel the seams of a hierarchized athletic gender binary—often described through the language of "unfair advantage," "legacy effects of testosterone," or simply "biological traits." Moreover, a trans feminist sports studies interrogates racialized medical paradigms of intersex variations wielded by the International Amateur Athletic Federation, now called World Athletics, and the International Olympic Committee that have blocked athletes such as Caster Semenya, Annet Negesa, Holarli Ativor, Francine Niyonsaba, Maria José Martinez-Patiño, Dutee

Chand, and Santhi Soundarajan from competition. Trans feminist sports studies rejects discursive and material forms of violence that situate women athletes within valuation matrices of femininity, athleticism, investment return, and other fetishized elements of extraction. Tools of trans feminist sports studies apply to athletes such as Serena Williams and Brittney Griner, for although they do not describe themselves as "trans" in an identificatory way, their racialized gender policing both within and outside feminist, anti-racist, and sports circles continues to mute recognition of their athletic excellence.

The contributions to this volume take up our call for a transfeminist sport studies in powerful and productive ways. Elizabeth Sharrow's essay brings a trans feminist sports studies lens to public policy making to explain how it is that we have arrived at a moment in which girls' and women's sport is used as a channel for anti-trans discourse. While recent trans exclusionary laws have accrued much interdisciplinary attention, Sharrow asserts that Title IX of the Education Amendment of 1972, a supposedly nondiscrimination law that is typically framed as feminist and inclusionary, yields insight into the current mobilization of transphobia and trans exclusion. In "Good Hair, Bad Math," Erica Rand homes in on the finer points of competitive pairs figure skating, a discipline in figure skating hallmarked by its hetero- and gender-normative dyad. Rand talks us through her gender-nonconforming figure skating pairs team, which, even with US Figure Skating's interpretive method of scoring criteria and unwritten codes of décolleté and "illusion fabric," manages to sustain its rule that "only pairs of the *same composition* [our emphasis] (woman and man, two women or two men) may compete against each other."[4] In a similar vein of pairing the seemingly unpairable, Tristan Venturi examines two other ostensibly disparate domains: sports and dating. Venturi delineates ideological similarities between activities of sports and dating that center the scrutiny of gendered bodies and illustrates a generative intellectual inquiry for trans feminist sports studies, one that asks what we might learn when we analyze sports alongside other realms of social and cultural production.

Imagining Sports Otherwise

In "The Athletic Issue" of *GLQ*, Mary Louise Adams (2013: 537) concluded her essay on the histories of gendered play vis-à-vis the third and fourth editions of the *Diagnostic and Statistical Manual of Mental Disorders*, arguing that "sport, as an institutionalized set of physical practices, the meaning of which is overdetermined, has little to offer to a queer physical culture." We might ask: what can sports possibly offer trans, nonbinary, and folks whose gender does not neatly fit into the fictitious binary that sports discourses naturalize? Despite anti-trans efforts from across the political spectrum, trans and gender-nonconforming people are using athletic settings to resist the conditions and institutions that seek to eliminate our place in sport. Jinsun Yang's article asks readers to suspend a political impulse of trans inclusion to explore how a nonbinary policy approach might be more fruitful in organized athletic events. Yang introduces the Queer Women Games, a nonbinary sports competition in Korea, as a glimpse of how athletes and organizers navigate gender norms when mainstream sporting organizations are not the arbiter of athletes' gender. Anima Adjepong extends this thread in their essay, "Queer African Feminist Orientations for a Trans Sports Studies," bringing a queer African feminism to bear on the field of trans sports studies. Adjepong enjoins feminist and trans sports studies scholars to shift away from a liberal individualist approach that characterizes much trans-inclusion-in-sports discourse, toward gender abolition. In the final piece of the "Sports Issue," members of Meninos Bons de Bola, Brazil's first trans soccer team, demand that trans access to sport be part of the broader struggle against repression and fascism in Brazil. Their manifesto speaks to the urgency of centering marginalized trans people within LGBT politics and against a political epicenter of right-wing extremism in Brazil.

The essays in this special issue underscore our conviction that sport participation is a vital component of trans feminist political projects and remind us that engaging in sports or other physical activity can in fact be a means to explore, refine, and affirm our gendered flesh on our own terms. It is our hope that readers of the "Sports Issue" find inspiration here for their own efforts to negotiate physical realms of competition and play in ever more liberatory ways.

CJ Jones is a PRODiG Postdoctoral Fellow at Purchase College and is currently working on a book manuscript tentatively titled "Governing Bodies: Trans Politics, Embodiment, and Critique in Sports."

Travers is professor of sociology at Simon Fraser University. Their recent book, *The Trans Generation: How Trans Kids (and Their Parents) Are Creating a Gender Revolution* (2018), situates trans kids in Canada and the United States, white settler nations characterized by significant social inequality.

Notes

1. Indiana House of Representatives, Participation in School Sports, HB 1041, 2022 Regular Session, introduced January 4, 2022, https://iga.in.gov/legislative/2022/bills/house/1041/#digest-heading.
2. Rugby Canada and Rugby USA are among several national associations that refused to follow World Rugby's lead in prohibiting transgender women from playing in women's competitions.
3. Trans activists and scholars refer to anti-trans feminists as trans-exclusionary radical feminists, or TERFs, a moniker such feminists resist, insisting they are not anti-trans people per se but rather critical of claims that transgender women are women and that inclusion in women's spaces is therefore a human right. Hateful rhetoric that characterizes

transgender women as "male" interlopers in women's spaces based on essentialist assumptions about sex/gender identity has a long history in feminist scholarship. See, for example, Raymond 1979.

4.   In December 2022 Skate Canada changed its regulations to allow for pairs of any gender to compete together (Marsten and Gul 2022).

References

Adams, Mary Louise. 2013. "No Taste for Rough-and-Tumble Play: Sport Discourses, the DSM, and the Regulation of Effeminacy." In "The Athletic Issue," edited by Jennifer Doyle. Special issue, *GLQ* 19, no 4: 515–43.

Bey, Marquis. 2022. *Black Trans Feminism*. Durham, NC: Duke University Press.

Butler, Judith. 2021. "Why Is the Idea of 'Gender' Provoking Backlash the World Over?" *Guardian*, October 23. https://www.theguardian.com/us-news/commentisfree/2021/oct/23/judith -butler-gender-ideology-backlash.

Carrington, Ben, and Ian McDonald, eds. 2009. *Marxism, Cultural Studies, and Sport*. Routledge Critical Studies in Sport. New York: Routledge.

Carter, Thomas F. 2008. *The Quality of Home Runs: The Passion, Politics, and Language of Cuban Baseball*. Durham, NC: Duke University Press.

Cavanagh, Sheila L., and Heather Sykes. 2006. "Transsexual Bodies at the Olympics: The International Olympic Committee's Policy on Transsexual Athletes at the 2004 Athens Summer Games." *Body and Society* 12, no. 3: 75–102.

Collins, Tony. 2013. *Sport in Capitalist Society: A Short History*. New York: Routledge.

Douglas, Delia D. 2005. "Venus, Serena, and the Women's Tennis Association: When and Where 'Race' Enters." *Sociology of Sport Journal* 22, no. 3: 256–82.

Douglas, Delia D. 2012. "Venus, Serena, and the Inconspicuous Consumption of Blackness: A Commentary on Surveillance, Race Talk, and New Racism(s)." *Journal of Black Studies* 43, no. 2: 127–45.

Dreger, Alice Domurat. 2000. *Hermaphrodites and the Medical Invention of Sex*. Cambridge, MA: Harvard University Press.

Enke, Finn. 2012. "Introduction: Transfeminist Perspectives." In *Transfeminist Perspectives: In and Beyond Transgender and Gender Studies*, edited by Finn Enke, 1–15. Philadelphia: Temple University Press.

Fair Play for Women. n.d. Homepage. https://fairplayforwomen.com (accessed January 20, 2020).

Fausto-Sterling, Anne. 2020. *Sexing the Body: Gender Politics and the Construction of Sexuality*. 2nd ed. New York: Basic.

Fine, Cordelia. 2017. *Testosterone Rex: Myths of Sex, Science, and Society*. New York: W. W. Norton.

Gill-Peterson, Jules. 2021. "The Anti-trans Lobby's Real Agenda." *Jewish Currents*, April 27. https:// jewishcurrents.org/the-anti-trans-lobbys-real-agenda.

Gleaves, John, and Tim Lehrbach. 2016. "Beyond Fairness: The Ethics of Inclusion for Transgender and Intersex Athletes." *Journal of the Philosophy of Sport* 43, no. 2: 311–26.

Hargreaves, Jennifer. 2013. "Gender Equality in Olympic Sport: A Brief History of Women's Setbacks and Successes at the Summer Olympic Games." *Aspetar Sports Medicine Journal* 2, no. 1: 80–86.

Higginbotham, Evelyn Brooks. 1992. "African-American Women's History and the Metalanguage of Race." *Signs* 17, no. 2: 251–74.

Jones, CJ. 2021. "Unfair Advantage Discourse in USA Powerlifting: Toward a Transfeminist Sports Studies." *TSQ* 8, no. 1: 58–74.

Koyama, Emi. 2003. "The Transfeminist Manifesto." In *Catching a Wave: Reclaiming Feminism for the Twenty-First Century*, edited by Rory Dicker and Alison Piepmeier, 244–61. Boston: Northeastern University Press.

Marsten, Emily, and Monika Gul. 2022. "Skate Canada Removes Gender Barrier in Pairs Skating." *CityNews 1130* (Vancouver), December 14. https://vancouver.citynews.ca/2022/12/14/skate-canada-gender-barrier-pairs/.

Pape, Madeleine. 2017. "The Fairest of Them All: Gender-Determining Institutions and the Science of Sex Testing." In *Gender Panic, Gender Policy*, edited by Vasilikie Demos and Marcia Texler Segal, 177–200. Advances in Gender Research 24. Bingley, UK: Emerald.

Pieper, Lindsay Parks. 2016. *Sex Testing: Gender Policing in Women's Sports*. Urbana: University of Illinois Press.

Pronger, Brian. 1990. *The Arena of Masculinity: Sports, Homosexuality, and the Meaning of Sex*. New York: St. Martin's Press.

Puar, Jasbir K. 2007. *Terrorist Assemblages: Homonationalism in Queer Times*. Durham, NC: Duke University Press.

Raymond, Janice G. 1979. *The Transsexual Empire: The Making of the She-Male*. Boston: Beacon.

Save Women's Sports. n.d. "About." https://savewomenssports.com/about-us-1 (accessed July 26, 2021).

Sharrow, Elizabeth A. 2021. "Sports, Transgender Rights, and the Bodily Politics of Cisgender Supremacy." *Laws* 10, no. 3: 63.

Stryker, Susan, and Talia M. Bettcher. 2016. "Introduction." *TSQ* 3, nos. 1–2: 5–14.

Travers. 2022. "Sport, Transgender Athletes, and Nonbinary Experience." In *The Oxford Handbook of Sport and Society*, edited by Lawrence A. Wenner, 924–28. New York: Oxford University Press.

Weheliye, Alexander G. 2014. *Habeas Viscus: Racializing Assemblages, Biopolitics, and Black Feminist Theories of the Human*. Durham, NC: Duke University Press.

Wolff, Michelle, David A. Rubin, and Amanda Lock Swarr. 2022. "The Intersex Issue: An Introduction." In "The Intersex Issue," edited by Michelle Wolff, David A. Rubin, and Amanda Lock Swarr. Special issue, *TSQ* 9, no. 2: 143–59.

Wynter, Sylvia. 2003. "Unsettling the Coloniality of Being/Power/Truth/Freedom: Towards the Human, after Man, Its Overrepresentation—An Argument." *CR: The New Centennial Review* 3, no. 3: 257–337.

Public Policy as Trans Harm

Troubling Administrative Governance through Transfeminist Sports Studies

ELIZABETH SHARROW

Abstract The observation that systems of state governance are more apt to do harm or violence to transgender and gender-diverse people is foundational to the field of trans studies. This article argues that public policy—including policy design, implementation, governance, and administration—is an important target for transfeminist sports studies. It illustrates the importance of attending to Title IX of the Education Amendments of 1972, a federal sex nondiscrimination policy in the United States. This case underscores how public policy through its widespread enactment in American school-sponsored sports and overreliance on binary logics of sex-segregated categories remains paramount, though underanalyzed, as a vehicle for trans harm.
Keywords Title IX, public policy, sex segregation

As of mid-April 2023, twenty-one US states have passed laws that constrain participation in interscholastic or intercollegiate athletics to cisgender students.[1] Although none of them nominally reference transgender or gender-diverse (or "trans") athletes, the mandates ban their participation on the school-sponsored team consistent with their gender identity if it differs from the sex they were assigned at birth (MAP 2023a). The laws intentionally delimit sex assigned at birth as the only valid identity classification for competitive athletic eligibility, conflating designations on birth certificates assigned based on infants' secondary sex traits with categories used to organize sports. As Governor Ron DeSantis signed one such bill, Florida's "Fairness in Women's Sports Act," into law, he declared, "Girls are going to play girls' sports and boys are going to play boys' sports . . . we're going to go based on biology, not based on ideology when we're doing sports" (Bloch 2021). When asked about the significance of signing the bill on the first day of LGBTQ+ Pride Month, DeSantis claimed, "It's not a message to anything other than saying we're going to protect fairness."

These state laws, and the hundreds of bills proposing similar policies introduced in legislatures over the past four years, represent several evolving

TSQ: Transgender Studies Quarterly ★ Volume 10, Number 2 ★ May 2023
DOI 10.1215/23289252-10440748   © 2023 Duke University Press

trends. Chiefly, and through the lens of sports studies, they are another flashpoint in the long history of institutionalized policing of participants in the women's category of competitive sport (Karkazis et al. 2012; Pieper 2016). Although the regulatory tactics of the recent state laws shift away from sex testing and hormonal regulation employed by international sports governance groups for nearly the past century (see Jordan-Young and Karkazis 2019; Posbergh 2022), exclusionary state laws are the most recent evolution in technologies of bodily policing that selectively mobilize the competitive athletic category for girls and women to target trans and gender-diverse people for exclusion.[2] State laws now authorize increased surveillance of identity documents, genitals, hormones, and gender presentation, targeting those girls and women who are, or who are perceived by others to be, gender transgressive (see further description in Sharrow 2021b). Furthermore, the logics at the core of these new laws reify the sex-segregated structures endemic to sport in their hyperreliance on binary, sex-based categories to organize competitive athletics (Schultz 2022; Sharrow 2017). Their described aims are to retain segregated structures under purported auspices of "fairness," irrespective of the consequent harms.

Yet these developments are also evidence of powerful political trends. As much as sports studies informs one perspective on the development of these laws, the field must also confront the important question of why sports are a key venue for anti-trans rhetoric. This article argues that research in "transfeminist sports studies" (see Jones 2021) must grapple with, and will be strengthened by engaging, the role of state authority in anti-trans discourses, laws, and public policies. Certainly, the explicitly trans-exclusionary trends in recent state lawmaking are an obvious case for interdisciplinary thinking that bring together critical perspectives on public policy, gender studies, and athletics. But so too are the seemingly inclusionary nondiscrimination laws like Title IX of the Education Amendments of 1972 that buttress sports governance through educational civil rights.[3]

On the one hand, Title IX has dramatically altered the American educational and sporting landscapes ensuring millions of athletic opportunities on teams for girls and women (Staurowsky et al. 2022). On the other hand, only some of those teams were ever inclusive of out trans or nonbinary athletes. Title IX encouraged growth in school-sponsored sports via sex-segregated teams (Sharrow 2017). In early April 2023 (while this article was in page proofs), the US Department of Education announced proposed changes to Title IX regulations regarding student eligibility on athletic teams (OCR 2023). The proposed regulations are open for public comment until early May and will not be finalized for some months; when finalized, they will represent formal policy on the rights of trans or nonbinary athletes to participate in segregated structures.[4] The proposal suggests that while schools, colleges, or universities cannot "categorically ban transgender students from participating on sports teams consistent with their gender identity" under

Title IX, "sex-related criteria that limit participation of some transgender students may be permitted, in some cases, when they enable the school to achieve an important educational objective, such as fairness in competition" (US DOE 2023). Thus it remains unclear how much trans eligibility will ultimately be delegated to states and sports governance organizations. In some states, either state law or state high school athletic association policies generate pathways for trans youth to participate in extant interscholastic teams. In others, state law excludes them. At the college level, collegiate governing bodies like the NCAA are left to determine trans eligibility in intercollegiate sports. In spring 2022, the NCAA abruptly announced a change to their long-standing trans inclusion guidelines, devolving inclusionary standards to the nongovernmental, elite sports governing agencies for each individual sport. On balance, administrative governance at all levels of the American state, in both specifics and vagaries, occludes trans autonomy.

Following the impulse behind CJ Jones and Travers's vision for "transfeminist sports studies" to "make strange" the "practices, systems, and structures . . . that pathologize transness in sports" (Jones 2021: 60), I argue we must bring critical perspectives to bear on Title IX (as currently interpreted) as a vehicle for trans harm. That is, Title IX, despite all that it has done to increase athletic opportunity for girls and women, remains problematic because of the way that it organizes governance of equality through sex segregation. Segregation, with its overt regulatory and administrative reliance on ideas about embodied "sex difference," authorizes both ideological damages and material exclusions against trans, non-binary, and gender-diverse people. In practice, the tactics used by federal policy-makers to address androcentrism in school-sponsored sports (i.e., incentivizing sex segregated teams for girls and women where schools had previously denied them) now serve as fodder for those who aim to forestall gendered equality that fulsomely includes trans people. Civil rights approaches to gendered equality in education, and athletic programming specifically, remain a public policy outlier—compared to other realms addressing discrimination on the basis of race, sex, or disability—in promoting sex segregation as the purportedly "nondiscriminatory" policy design (McDonagh and Pappano 2007; Sharrow 2021a). In this article, I urge scholars to take seriously the role of governmental structures—not merely sporting institutions—in promoting troubling and incomplete vehicles for trans inclusion in sport through a purportedly emancipatory rights-based model. Further, although recent state exclusionary laws demand scholarly critique, so too does the administrative capacity of quotidian liberal feminist "solutions" to sex discrimination that produce trans harm under auspices of "fairness" in the status quo.[5] The emergent field of transfeminist sports studies, in its evolving intersections with trans studies and political science (as well as related disciplines), has the possibility of providing insights that could help recraft both sports and civil rights governance to avoid the enforcement of binary logics (and attendant notions of "normal bodies") if scholarship attends to the power and increasing caprice of the administrative state.

Why Center Politics in Studies of Sports?

First, it is important to contextualize recent anti-trans sports policies in US politics and political discourse. Politically, trans identities and trans rights are under scrutiny and outright attack from many directions. Anti-trans lawmaking over the past decade escalated in the context of persistent anti-trans animus within the American public (Flores et al. 2020; Lewis et al. 2017) and battles over federal authority among political elites. Decades of inaction by the US Congress on a federal Equality Act (historically referred to as an Employment Non-Discrimination Act, or ENDA) that would secure nondiscrimination protections for LGBTQ+ people accelerated the devolution of civil rights challenges to state legislatures (McNamara 2020; Vitulli 2010).[6] Sports moved to the center of political contestation on the heels of prior conservative lawmaking in some states that sought to limit access by transgender and gender-diverse people to public accommodations, including sex-segregated restrooms (Beauchamp 2019; Schilt and Westbrook 2015). In short, the lack of political consensus among lawmakers at the national level left a policy vacuum that was subsequently filled by legislators in the more ideologically polarized, conservative-led American state legislatures.

At the same time, many localities and some states passed laws that expanded trans rights (Taylor, Lewis, and Haider-Markel 2018). Despite an absence of congressional action, Obama-era federal executive agencies promulgated affirming, if fleeting, federal protections for trans people. For example, in 2016 under President Barack Obama's leadership, the US Departments of Justice and Education announced policy guidance to school administrators indicating that transgender students must be permitted access to bathrooms that aligned with their gender identity (OCR and CRD 2016). Yet the unsettled fate of federal LGBTQ+ protections created vulnerabilities. The Obama-era policy guidance did not carry the weight of federal law, enabling the successive administration under Donald Trump to withdraw the guidance. The Trump administration slowly revealed cross-agency policies aimed at blocking the recognition of gender-diverse people in federal-level policy implementation, a move the *New York Times* described as threatening to define transgender people "out of existence" (Green, Benner, and Pear 2018). Although Trump's successor, President Joe Biden, rescinded all Trump-era, anti-trans policies in the early days of his presidency, the Trump administration strategies would portend the subsequent political obsession with gender-diverse people exhibited by the conservative Right (see Sharrow 2021b).[7]

In the fight for legal rights for trans Americans, disputes over whether trans identity is biodetermined have accelerated the reliance on essentialist rhetoric among conservatives (Wuest 2019). In the wake of the Trump administration, state legislatures (particularly those controlled by Republican lawmakers) have become key sites for proto-fascist, right-wing lawmaking designed to contest federal authority over civil rights (Miras and Rouse 2022).[8] This recent flurry of anti-trans state legislative activity escalates right-wing political organizing pursuant to judicial rulings that secure "religious" protections for Americans hostile to LGBTQ+ people (Wuest 2021). Particularly as sports moved center stage in 2020 and 2021, both lawmakers and the mass public became steeped in biased and voluminous coverage by conservative media outlets that misrepresent trans life (January 2021; Paterson 2022), even as "mainstream" sources reported relatively little and often with inaccurate details about the stakes of trans athletic inclusion (Gingerich 2021). In sum, recent attacks on transgender athletes both exemplify and are firmly entrenched in the mounting political violence targeting marginalized groups (and trans people specifically) with the backing of state institutions.

Yet neither feminist sports studies nor recent political studies, either on their own, can explain precisely why we have witnessed this turn to expressly targeting the realm of interscholastic and intercollegiate sports. I argue that placing critical sports studies in conversation with trans studies on public policy and politics provides fertile ground to deepen our understanding of this moment. In particular, transfeminist sport studies (Jones 2021) at the intersection of trans studies and political science/policy studies is poised to productively scrutinize the convergence of gendered policing, technologies of administrative power, and the cultural discourses in and around sports that demarcate it as a site of, and for, political violence against transgender people.[9] On the heels of law-making attempts to deny trans and gender diverse people access to public restrooms and locker-room facilities, sports exist in a policy context that, by dint of its reliance on strict sex segregation, remains vulnerable to the mobilization of transphobia and transmisogyny. Foundational, though often unarticulated assumptions about cisgender status are core to purportedly inclusive policy governance in school-sponsored sports, and they are increasingly being mobilized to exclude gender-diverse athletes from segregated athletics under the auspices of "fairness" (Jones 2021; Sharrow 2021b).

My intervention aims to create space to ask: what work does the overt politicization of spaces for "play and leisure" do to entrench oppression to trans, nonbinary, and gender-diverse people? Notably, sports have often served (even as they simultaneously obscure) the broader conservative political projects of, for example, fostering nationalism, addressing racism in merely symbolic ways, and promoting neoliberalism (Luther and Davidson 2020; Zirin 2009). I offer that theorizing transfeminist sport studies through policy and politics allows us to consider why sports are emerging as a key racialized and gendered political battleground. Asking "why sports?" (and targeting trans people through sports) enlarges the sports studies conversation to encompass questions often situated more squarely in public policy and administration studies or in political science. At the same time, analyzing "why sports" in this ideological moment also expands the terrain of political study to include purported "leisure" space (as sports are commonly framed as such). Interdisciplinary critique reveals important questions that, I argue, can advance knowledge in trans studies, the social sciences, policy studies, gender studies, and sports studies. Similarly, a focus on the politics of sport in transfeminist perspective has urgent applications. Previous challenges to anti-trans "bathroom bans" from trans and intersectional-feminist perspectives gave rise to analyses effectively challenging sex-segregated restrooms (Davis 2014, 2018). Such critiques that take seriously the political and public policy contexts in transfeminist sports studies will be well poised to effectively challenge the deployment of binary sex categories to reject trans and gender-diverse people in sport.

Finally, absent analyses of these public policy contexts, critical perspectives in transfeminist sport studies might misapprehend important institutions for critique. Although human rights frameworks are often asserted as important vehicles for full inclusion of trans athletes in sport (Cunningham, Isard, and Melton 2021; Mitra and Karkazis 2020), less attention is given to the existing civil rights policies that determine current practice. Systems of governance that implement nondiscrimination public policy are particularly harmful to trans populations in sports precisely because they are authorized by the state. The aforementioned reliance on sex segregated logics for athletics in federal policy guidance, and the simultaneous lack of policy interpretations that stipulate how to include gender-diverse people in segregated structures reveal the ways that administrative violence can operate through both the actions and inactions of state authority. Transfeminist sports studies should keep state institutions–including legislatures, courts, bureaucracies and public policies–core to future critique. Next, I illustrate the importance of this claim by illustrating the connections between trans studies critiques of governance, and Title IX.

Why Center Public Policy in Transfeminist Sports Studies?

Critiquing state actions (and the nation-state itself) by illustrating its many harms on trans subjectivities is foundational to trans studies. It is necessary "to criticize the workings of institutions, which appear to be both neutral and independent; to criticize them in such a manner that the political violence which has always exercised itself obscurely through them . . . so that one can fight against them" (Foucault, in Chomsky and Foucault 2006: 41). Trans legal scholars who have followed this path reveal the negative impacts of denying gender-diverse people access to accurate identification documents, public facilities, workplace nondiscrimination protections, or medical care (Currah 2008, 2022; Currah and Moore 2008; Davis 2014; Spade 2008, 2011). Trans harm is often enabled, rather than ameliorated, by systems of governance (Stanley 2021).[10]

Certainly, policy-centered critique is already an active component of trans sports studies. Yet such scholarship is most apt to critique sports policies developed by sports governance organizations (Jones 2021; Posbergh 2022; Travers 2009). Problematizing sports policies provides urgently needed perspectives on the selective targeting and policing of athletic girls and women by sports governance. But gendered public policies—i.e., policies developed by and for the realm of state governance—are less commonly problematized in sports studies, despite their equally pivotal roles (Griffin 2012; Sharrow 2021a). Absent the teachings of trans studies on the harms and exclusion enacted by public policies, sports studies might undertheorize the foundational role that public policy design, implementation, and administration can play in the oppression and domination of trans people.

Transfeminist sports studies will benefit from attending to the "work that sex does" (Currah 2022) in sports-related public policies, though scholarship in that vein is currently limited. In the final section of this article, I briefly illustrate what can be gained from engaging literatures on public policy and public administration. Here, I offer a unique perspective on Title IX. I argue that both federal policy context under Title IX, and the aforementioned gaps and insufficiencies of a federalized structure in the United States, creates critical vulnerabilities and structural fissures. These structural problems open space for anti-trans policy-making which then negatively overdetermines outcomes in the realm of sports for trans people due, perhaps unexpectedly, to policy design itself.

Transfeminist Sports Policy Studies? The Case of Title IX

I focus on public policy to scrutinize its role in excluding and harming trans athletes in order to expose one engine of gendered domination in US sport. Nominally, Title IX is a sex nondiscrimination civil rights policy in the realm of education. Over the past half-century, its implementation has renegotiated the terms of educational access, including access to extracurricular activities like school-sponsored sports. Because Title IX functions as a national public policy, its logics determine the participation experiences of thousands of students each year. Nearly 8 million high school students and over five hundred thousand college students participate in interscholastic and intercollegiate sports annually (NFHS 2019; NCAA 2021). However, athletic opportunity under Title IX is heavily structured by sex-segregated teams. Sex segregation, enshrined in policy design by federal policy makers in the 1970s, is now thoroughly naturalized as standard practice in American high schools, colleges, and universities under Title IX (Sharrow 2017).

The historic customs that gave rise to this design was built on two important assumptions. First, policymakers assumed that absent policy intervention that forced schools to create new teams "for" girls and women the long-standing practices that favored school-sponsored teams "for" boys and men were unlikely to change. Discrimination against girls and women placed them at a chronic disadvantage for coaching, skill development, strength and conditioning, and other supports that might have made them competitive for preexisting (men's) teams. Second, policymakers assumed that assigning individuals to either "boy's" or "girl's" teams would be straightforward for both administrators and the athletes themselves (see Sharrow 2017).

Over fifty years into Title IX's implementation, these assumptions no longer hold. As this article goes to print, federal policymakers have merely stipulated new draft regulations on the responsibilities of school administrators in ensuring equal opportunity to trans and nonbinary athletes in a sex segregated model (US DOE 2023). The proposed guidance suggests a future marked by uneven outcomes for trans youth across states, municipalities, schools, and school districts, leaving trans youth vulnerable to social exclusion and diminished physical and mental health (Goldberg 2021). The outcome of federal administrative rule-making on athletic eligibility could engender bespoke rules for *excluding* trans athletes under auspices of "flexibility" for "ensuring fairness in competition or preventing sports-related injury" (US DOE 2023). The proposed rules fail to acknowledge their reliance on sex stereotypes embedded in the articulated fears of "injury." Ironically, eradicating sex stereotypes in education was a founding motivation of activists who pressed to pass Title IX in 1972 (Sharrow 2017).

At the same time, sex segregation goes largely unchallenged in policy and practice, itself a fraught policy design premised on "protecting" women from physical harm. Title IX enables windows of possibility for "integrated" teams only under certain conditions. Girls and women (presumed to be cisgender) must be granted a tryout for teams designated for boys and men only when a similar team for girls and women is lacking; sex-separate teams are overwhelmingly implemented in practice. "Sex integration" has at least the potential to unseat the naturalized logics of "necessary" sex segregation in sports. However, integration is disincentivized by public policy, which instead promotes a preference for sex-separate spheres (OCR 1979).[11]

Certainly, sports policies at all levels frequently engage sex-segregated categories. Critiques of sex-segregated athletic structures illustrate the ways that the embedded gendered logics overdetermine the categorization of competitive eligibility, thus limiting inclusion of trans and gender-diverse people and undermining full equality (Druckman and Sharrow forthcoming; McDonagh and Pappano 2007; Milner and Braddock 2016; Ring 2009; Sharrow 2021a; Travers 2011).[12] Yet little has changed to disrupt such structures in practice since Travers (2014: 194) anticipated that "current policy debate on transgender participation in mainstream sport questions the sex-segregated structure of sporting spaces." In years hence, the ongoing administration of segregation under Title IX and the lack of policy specificity for trans inclusion in that model has created space for neglect, at a minimum, and increasingly explicit trans harm.

Trans athletes face many challenges resulting from Title IX's policy history (not mere cultural or normative practice) that established sex-segregated athletics as a liberal feminist solution to the problem of sex discrimination in sports (see Sharrow 2017, 2021a; Brake 2010). Policy design calcified segregation. Administrative governance structures utilize sex-based categories that are uniquely rigid and widely employed in schools nationwide, all under the ethos of advancing civil rights. This segregated policy design used in sports under Title IX is puzzlingly strict in comparison to other gendered policy realms, including Title IX's applications in classroom settings where students are integrated "without regard to sex" (Sharrow 2021a: 3). Widespread critique of both policy and practice of sex-segregated classrooms has ensured that neither sex nor gender identity is a justification for exclusion (at least not per se) from learning environments in schools or colleges (English 2016; Williams 2016). In parallel contexts, policies have evolved to address evidence of harm. Many historically single-sex women's educational institutions now include transwomen (and other gender-diverse people), illustrating that institutional evolutions are possible with trans-inclusive vision (Nanney and Brunsma 2017). Segregated athletics would benefit from further engaging with such perspectives to envision possibilities for the future.

Yet public policy–centered analyses are equally urgent, given current events. Federal guidance remains in flux. The Biden administration's US Department of Education (DOE) announced that, pursuant to the interpretations of Title VII of the Civil Rights Act of 1964 in the *Bostock v. Clayton County* US Supreme Court case, gender identity protections as sex nondiscrimination would guide policy interpretations (US DOE 2021).[13] But this policy guidance issued by the DOE is now under scrutiny by the courts,[14] and in July 2022 a judge in Tennessee temporarily blocked its enforcement (Brink 2022a). In the same month, the DOE publicized that it would announce new draft rules (subject to public comment) specific to trans inclusion in athletics (Brink 2022b). These draft rules were only made public in April 2023. With future access to protections for trans athletes imperiled, federal policy could soon contrast with recently passed state laws, leaving the courts to potentially decide interpretation of Title IX and the fates of trans athletes. At the same time, it remains to be seen whether future policy guidance will also address the incorporation of nonbinary or gender-diverse students into a sex-segregated system. Perhaps, if lower court rulings—such as in the case challenging a trans-exclusionary law passed in Idaho in 2020—overturn state laws and are not further contested in higher courts, less overtly harmful federal guidelines on trans inclusion will follow (Kliegman 2020).[15] Yet any forthcoming policy guidelines seem unlikely to upend the structuring conditions of sex-segregated teams, at least not without mass mobilizations demanding such changes.[16] Future opportunities for trans athletes are more likely to require careful consideration for working around and through ostensibly "inclusionary" policy, a challenging task that transfeminist sports legal scholars might fruitfully engage (Buzuvis 2012, 2021). In the meantime, sex-segregated structures remain legal.

Conclusions

A public policy–centered analysis of recent politics would caution those organizing for trans inclusion against merely hoping for unilateral, uncontested policy change in a federalized system. The recent swell of anti-trans lawmaking at the state level is a political by-product of the American federalized lawmaking system in which parties lacking executive leadership or definitive legislative majorities (in this case, Republicans at the federal level in 2023) can seek legislative victories in the states where they retain majority status (Miras and Rouse 2022). At the same time, trans-exclusionary lawmaking is not merely partisan, it is also a political by-product of the athletic logics that both produce and cement segregation as a necessary condition for athletic equality. As illustrated in the comments by Governor DeSantis, state lawmakers are mobilizing fraught understandings of the purpose behind sex-segregated competitive spheres to enact many forms of trans harm under discourses of "fairness" that center cisgender athletes as the only rightful beneficiaries of nondiscrimination policy (see Sharrow 2021b). Transfeminist sports studies can provide the critical perspective and critique necessary to reveal the politics in such false framings. In these ways, a public policy–informed, transfeminist sports studies provides the tools necessary to pave the way in both sports and policy studies.

In sum, I hope this article might generate new interest in public policy–centered sports studies as one among many tools for transfeminisms. The structuring capacities of public policies often determine the quality of trans life in sports, as elsewhere, and transfeminist sports critique has the potential to apply its lessons and perspectives in parallel, nonsports contexts as well. Political theorists have long-articulated ambivalence about rights-based models for the full inclusion of marginalized groups in a democratic society (e.g., Brown 2000). Yet limited scholarship delineates the specific challenges presented to this model by athletic spheres (but see, e.g., Butler 1998; Hextrum and Sethi 2022). Still, in liberal political orders premised on incorporating historically marginalized groups via articulated rights, nominal "rights" to sport (whether secured through public policy reform or legal interpretation) are likely things that transgender, nonbinary, and gender-diverse people "cannot not want" (Brown 2000: 231). That is, even as trans people build communities and networks beyond and aside from state control, the rights afforded by state institutions are nevertheless impactful to their livelihood. Gender emancipatory, or gender abolitionist models for the future or sport may be more fruitful, but the given governmental frameworks are still likely to determine possibilities in the near future. Whatever the next short- or long-term steps, we must be attentive to the problematic logics of policy that will exacerbate trans (and all forms of gendered) harm without critique. And with gendered forms of exclusion poised to police gender-nonconforming cis people as well, there may be powerful allies available in the fight against trans harm if we frame the stakes as broadly as possible (Associated Press 2022). With analysis that applies trans-centered perspectives on the implementation and administration of civil rights in sport, this emerging field may to reveal the tensions and limits embedded in gendered struggles in sports and beyond.

Elizabeth Sharrow is associate professor of public policy and history at the University of Massachusetts Amherst. Their work examines the politics of public policy in the late twentieth- and early twenty-first-century United States with a specific focus on how policy shapes understandings and intersectional repertoires of sex and gender. They are coauthor of *Equality Unfulfilled: How Title IX's Policy Design Undermines Change To College Sport* (2023).

Acknowledgements

This essay benefited greatly from my conversations with Anna Baeth, Logan Casey, Bridgette Davis, Izzy Sederbaum, Dara Strolovitch, and Mara Toone. I thank them each for their care and friendship.

Notes

1. States with exclusionary laws as of April 12, 2023, include Alabama, Arizona, Arkansas, Florida, Idaho, Indiana, Iowa, Kansas, Kentucky, Louisiana, Mississippi, Montana, North Dakota, Oklahoma, South Carolina, South Dakota, Tennessee, Texas, Utah, West Virginia, and Wyoming. Temporary legal injunctions block enforcement in Idaho, Indiana, Utah, and West Virginia. A permanent court order blocks Montana's ban for collegiate sports but not for K–12 sports. See MAP 2023a for any additional updates that transpired after April 12.

2. Notably, at the international competitive level, athletes with intersex traits have been the most heavily targeted and policed in recent years (Karkazis et al. 2012). The most high-profile elite athletes recently targeted by policy have not publicly identified as trans (e.g., Caster Semenya). However, the logics of bodily investigation (i.e., hormone testing) invoked in international policies that target them have been employed by US state legislators for anti-trans policies. Trans inclusion policies in elite sport vary widely and are themselves swiftly evolving.

3. Title IX is a US federal civil rights statute that bans discrimination in education "on the basis of sex" (20 U.S.C. §1681). School-sponsored athletics are targeted by policy because they are component programs.

4. In June 2022, the US Department of Education promised to issue draft policy guidelines specific to trans athletic inclusion before the end of the year, a deadline they failed to meet. In the early months of 2023, legislators in over half of American states and in the US Congress proposed additional legislation to restrict access to school-sponsored sports for athletes based on their sex assigned at birth (Equality Federation 2023).

5. There is, of course, much to say about the loaded valence of this term in sports competition and categorization, too much in fact to cover in this short note. However, readers should consider Jones 2021, or Jordan-Young and Karkazis 2019 and Karkazis et al. 2012, among others for critical perspectives on the work this term does.

6.   This devolution unevenly impacted multiple realms of LGBTQ+ politics, including (but not limited to) workplace and housing nondiscrimination protections, rights at school, the ability to secure identity documents, and marriage rights (MAP 2017). In 2023, efforts to enshrine inequality in health care, education, and public life again escalated in both number and speed in nearly every statehouse in the country (MAP 2023b).

7.   Among Biden's first acts as president in January 2021 was to sign Executive Order 13988, which required a review of all policies on gender identity discrimination made under the Trump administration.

8.   From 2021 to 2023, this took the form of right-wing political (i.e., US Republican Party) backlash against a left-leaning (i.e., US Democratic Party) presidential administration.

9.   Other contexts reveal overlap among trans, feminist, political, and sports studies. For example, scholarship examines political responses to Colin Kaepernick's Black Lives Matter protests during National Football League games in public opinion (Towler, Crawford, and Bennet 2020), and the shifting cultural politics produced by the 1968 Mexico City Olympic protests of anti-Black policies (Hartmann 2003). Finally, feminist scholars demonstrate the imbricated gendered histories of political organizing and sports arenas (Schultz 2019; Ware 2011; Cahn 1995; Enke 2007).

10.   See also parallel analyses of how educational institutions (Woolley 2015; Riggs and Bartholomaeus 2018) and medical science (Fausto-Sterling 2000; Malatino 2019; Shuster 2021) also enact such violence.

11.   Scholars demonstrate the harmful impacts on trans athletes of all ages in necessary efforts to assimilate into this dominant system (Travers 2016).

12.   The harms of segregation on trans athletes are certainly noted by scholars (Travers 2009, 2011), though less frequently analyzed in public policies.

13.   *Bostock v. Clayton County*, 590 US_(2020).

14.   Similar interpretations are evident in legal decisions on cases contesting bans on trans youths' accessing school restrooms that affirm their gender identity (Natanson 2021).

15.   Currently, the court case (*Hecox v. Little*) contesting the Idaho trans sports ban—the first of its kind—has prevented the implementation of the Idaho law even as the ruling is subject to appeal.

16.   See also Druckman and Sharrow (forthcoming) on the structural and institutional threats to potential mobilizations.

References

Associated Press. 2022. "Utah Officials Secretly Investigated Female Athlete's Gender." August 18. https://www.usnews.com/news/politics/articles/2022-08-18/utah-officials-secretly-looked-into-female-athletes-gender.

Beauchamp, Toby. 2019. *Going Stealth: Transgender Politics and U.S. Surveillance Practices*. Durham, NC: Duke University Press.

Bloch, Emily. 2021. "DeSantis Signs Controversial Transgender Girls Sports Ban on First Day of Pride in Jacksonville." *Florida Times-Union*, June 1. https://www.jacksonville.com/story/news/education/2021/06/01/florida-gov-ron-desantis-signs-controversial-transgender-girls-sports-ban-1st-day-pride-jacksonville/5289975001/.

Brake, Deborah. 2010. *Getting in the Game: Title IX and the Women's Sports Revolution*. New York: New York University Press.

Brink, Meghan. 2022a. "Federal Judge Blocks Title IX Guidance on Transgender Students." *Inside Higher Ed*, July 19. https://www.insidehighered.com/news/2022/07/19/federal-judge-blocks-ed-dept-title-ix-guidance-trans-students.

Brink, Meghan. 2022b. "Protections for Trans Athletes in Title IX Proposal Still Unknown." *Inside Higher Ed*, July 5. https://www.insidehighered.com/news/2022/07/05/title-ix-transgender-athletes-be-considered-separately.

Brown, Wendy. 2000. "Suffering Rights as Paradoxes." *Constellations* 7, no. 2: 230–41.

Butler, Judith. 1998. "Athletic Genders: Hyperbolic Instance and/or the Overcoming of Sexual Binarism." *Stanford Humanities Review* 6, no. 2: 103–11.

Buzuvis, Erin. 2012. "Including Transgender Athletes in Sex-Segregated Sport." In *Sexual Orientation and Gender Identity in Sport: Essays from Activists, Coaches, and Scholars*, edited by George B. Cunningham, 23–34. College Station, TX: Center for Sport Management Research and Education.

Buzuvis, Erin. 2021. "Law, Policy, and the Participation of Transgender Athletes in the United States." *Sport Management Review* 24, no. 3: 439–51.

Cahn, Susan. 1995. *Coming on Strong: Gender and Sexuality in Twentieth-Century Women's Sport.* Cambridge, MA: Harvard University Press.

Chomsky, Noam, and Michel Foucault. 2006. *The Chomsky-Foucault Debate: On Human Nature.* New York: The New Press.

Cunningham, George B., Risa Isard, and E. Nicole Melton. 2021. "Transgender Inclusion in Sport." *Kinesiology Review* 11, no. 1: 64–70.

Currah, Paisley. 2008. "Expecting Bodies: The Pregnant Man and Transgender Exclusion from the Employment Non-Discrimination Act." *WSQ* 36, nos. 3–4: 330–36.

Currah, Paisley. 2022. *Sex Is as Sex Does: Governing Transgender Identity.* New York: New York University Press.

Currah, Paisley, and Lisa Jean Moore. 2008. "'We Won't Know Who You Are': Contesting Sex Designations in New York City Birth Certificates." *Hypatia* 24, no. 3: 113–35.

Davis, Heath Fogg. 2014. "Sex-Classification Policies as Transgender Discrimination: An Intersectional Critique." *Perspectives on Politics* 12, no. 1: 45–60.

Davis, Heath Fogg. 2018. "Why the 'Transgender' Bathroom Controversy Should Make Us Rethink Sex-Segregated Public Bathrooms." *Politics, Groups, and Identities* 6, no. 2: 199–216.

Druckman, James N., and Elizabeth A. Sharrow. Forthcoming. *Equality Unfulfilled: How Title IX's Policy Design Undermines Change to College Sports.* Cambridge: Cambridge University Press.

English, Ashley. 2016. "Rewriting Title IX: The Department of Education's Response to Feminists' Comments in the Rulemaking Process." *Politics and Gender* 12, no. 3: 491–517.

Enke, Finn. 2007. *Finding the Movement: Sexuality, Contested Space, and Feminist Activism.* Durham, NC: Duke University Press.

Equality Federation. 2023. "Bill Tracker: Anti-Transgender Student Athletics." https://www.equalityfederation.org/tracker/anti-transgender-student-athletics (accessed March 22, 2023).

Fausto-Sterling, Anne. 2000. *Sexing the Body: Gender Politics and the Construction of Sexuality.* New York: Basic.

Flores, Andrew R., Donald P. Haider-Markel, Daniel C. Lewis, Patrick R. Miller, Barry L. Tadlock, and Jami K. Taylor. 2020. "Public Attitudes about Transgender Participation in Sports: The Roles of Gender, Gender Identity Conformity, and Sports Fandom." *Sex Roles* 83, nos. 5–6: 382–98.

Gingerich, Mia. 2021. "National TV News Fails to Mention Texas' Trans Youth Sports Ban." Media Matters for America, October 13. https://www.mediamatters.org/justice-civil-liberties/national-tv-news-fails-mention-texas-trans-youth-sports-ban-which.

Goldberg, Shoshana. 2021. "Fair Play: The Importance of Sports Participation for Transgender Youth." Washington, DC: Center for American Progress.

Green, Erica, Katie Benner, and Robert Pear. 2018. "'Transgender' Could Be Defined out of Existence under Trump Administration." *New York Times*, October 21. https://www.nytimes.com/2018/10/21/us/politics/transgender-trump-administration-sex-definition.html.

Griffin, Pat. 2012. "'Ain't I a Woman?': Transgender and Intersex Student Athletes in Women's Collegiate Sports." In *Transfeminist Perspectives: In and beyond Transgender and Gender Studies*, edited by Anne Enke, 98–111. Philadelphia: Temple University Press.

Hartmann, Douglas. 2003. *Race, Culture, and the Revolt of the Black Athlete: The 1968 Olympic Protests and Their Aftermath*. Chicago: University of Chicago Press.

Hextrum, Kirsten, and Simran Sethi. 2022. "Title IX at 50: Legitimating State Domination of Women's Sport." *International Review for the Sociology of Sport* 57, no. 2: 655–72.

January, Brianna. 2021. "Fox News Has Aired More Segments on Trans Athletes so Far in 2021 than It Did in the Last Two Years Combined." Media Matters for America, May 3. https://www.mediamatters.org/fox-news/fox-news-has-aired-more-segments-trans-athletes-so-far-2021-it-did-last-two-years-combined.

Jones, CJ. 2021. "Unfair Advantage Discourse in USA Powerlifting: Toward a Transfeminist Sports Studies." *TSQ* 8, no. 1: 58–74.

Jordan-Young, Rebecca, and Katrina Karkazis. 2019. *Testosterone: An Unauthorized Biography*. Cambridge, MA: Harvard University Press.

Karkazis, Katrina, Rebecca Jordan-Young, Georgiann Davis, and Silvia Camporesi. 2012. "Out of Bounds? A Critique of the New Policies on Hyperandrogenism in Elite Female Athletes." *American Journal of Bioethics* 12, no. 7: 3–16.

Kliegman, Julie. 2020. "Idaho Banned Trans Athletes from Women's Sports; She's Fighting Back." *Sports Illustrated*, June 30. https://www.si.com/sports-illustrated/2020/06/30/idaho-transgender-ban-fighting-back.

Lewis, Daniel, Andrew Flores, Donald Haider-Markel, Patrick Miller, Barry Tadlock, and Jami Taylor. 2017. "Degrees of Acceptance: Variation in Public Attitudes toward Segments of the LGBT Community." *Political Research Quarterly* 70, no. 4: 861–75.

Luther, Jessica, and Kavitha Davidson. 2020. *Loving Sports When They Don't Love You Back: Dilemmas of the Modern Fan*. Austin: University of Texas Press.

Malatino, Hil. 2019. *Queer Embodiment: Monstrosity, Medical Violence, and Intersex Experience*. Lincoln: University of Nebraska Press.

MAP (Movement Advancement Project). 2017. "Mapping Transgender Equality in the United States." https://www.lgbtmap.org/mapping-trans-equality (accessed March 16, 2023).

MAP (Movement Advancement Project). 2023a. "Equality Maps: Bans on Transgender Youth Participation in Sports." https://www.lgbtmap.org/equality-maps/sports_participation_bans (accessed April 12, 2023).

MAP (Movement Advancement Project). 2023b. *Under Fire: The War on LGBTQ People in America*. https://www.mapresearch.org/under-fire-report (accessed March 22, 2023).

McDonagh, Eileen, and Laura Pappano. 2007. *Playing with the Boys: Why Separate Is Not Equal in Sports*. New York: Oxford University Press.

McNamara, Kelly. 2020. "Failing to Protect: A Historical Analysis of The Employment Nondiscrimination Act." *Sociological Spectrum* 40, no. 4: 269–88.

Milner, Adrienne N., and Jomills Henry Braddock. 2016. *Sex Segregation in Sports: Why Separate Is Not Equal*. New York: Praeger.

Miras, Nicholas S., and Stella M. Rouse. 2022. "Partisan Misalignment and the Counter-Partisan Response: How National Politics Conditions Majority-Party Policy Making in the American States." *British Journal of Political Science* 52, no. 2: 573–92.

Mitra, Payshni, and Katrina Karkazis. 2020. "'They're Chasing Us away from Sport': Human Rights Violations in Sex Testing of Elite Women Athletes." New York: Human Rights Watch.

Nanney, Megan, and David L. Brunsma. 2017. "Moving beyond Cis-Terhood: Determining Gender through Transgender Admittance Policies at U.S. Women's Colleges." *Gender and Society* 31, no. 2: 145–70.

Natanson, Virginia. 2021. "Virginia School Board Will Pay $1.3 Million in Settlement to Transgender Student Gavin Grimm, Who Sued over Bathroom Policy." *Washington Post*, August 26. https://www.washingtonpost.com/local/education/transgender-bathroom-settlement -gavin-grimm/2021/08/26/0f186784-0699-11ec-a266-7c7fe02fa374_story.html.

NCAA (National Collegiate Athletic Association). 2021. "NCAA Sports Sponsorship and Parti-cipation Rates Report, 2021." Indianapolis: National Collegiate Athletic Association.

NFHS (National Federation of High Schools). 2019. "2018–19 High School Athletics Participation Survey." High School Participation Survey Archive. https://www.nfhs.org/media/1020412 /2018–19_participation_survey.pdf.

OCR (Office for Civil Rights, US Department of Education). 1979. "A Policy Interpretation: Title IX and Intercollegiate Athletics." *Federal Register* 44, no. 239. http://www2.ed.gov/about /offices/list/ocr/docs/t9interp.html.

OCR (Office for Civil Rights, US Department of Education) and CRD (Civil Rights Division, US Department of Justice). 2016. "Dear Colleague Letter: Transgender Students." http://www2 .ed.gov/about/offices/list/ocr/letters/colleague-201605-title-ix-transgender.pdf (accessed March 16, 2023).

Paterson, Alex. 2022. "'Doom and Groom': Fox News Has Aired 170 Segments Discussing Trans People in the Past Three Weeks." Media Matters for America, April 8. https://www.media matters.org/fox-news/doom-groom-fox-news-has-aired-170-segments-discussing-trans -people-past-three-weeks.

Pieper, Lindsay Parks. 2016. *Sex Testing: Gender Policing in Women's Sports*. Urbana: University of Illinois Press.

Posbergh, Anna. 2022. "Defining 'Woman': A Governmentality Analysis of How Protective Policies Are Created in Elite Women's Sport." *International Review for the Sociology of Sport* 57, no. 8: 1350–70.

Riggs, Damien W., and Clare Bartholomaeus. 2018. "Cisgenderism and Certitude: Parents of Transgender Children Negotiating Educational Contexts." *TSQ* 5, no. 1: 67–82.

Ring, Jennifer. 2009. *Stolen Bases: Why American Girls Don't Play Baseball*. Urbana: University of Illinois Press.

Schilt, Kristen, and Laurel Westbrook. 2015. "Bathroom Battlegrounds and Penis Panics." *Contexts* 14, no. 3: 26–31.

Schultz, Jaime. 2019. "More than Fun and Games: Cell Sixteen, Female Liberation, and Physical Competence; or, Why Sport Matters." *International Journal of the History of Sport* 36, nos. 17–18: 1552–73.

Schultz, Jaime. 2022. "Sex Segregation in Elite Sport: What's the Problem?" In *Gender Diversity and Sport: Interdisciplinary Perspectives*, edited by Gemma Witcomb and Elizabeth Peel, 13–33. London: Taylor and Francis.

Sharrow, Elizabeth A. 2017. "'Female Athlete' Politic: Title IX and the Naturalization of Sex Difference in Public Policy." *Politics, Groups, and Identities* 5, no. 1: 46–66.

Sharrow, Elizabeth A. 2021a. "Sex Segregation as Policy Problem: A Gendered Policy Paradox." *Politics, Groups, and Identities* 9, no. 2: 258–79.

Sharrow, Elizabeth A. 2021b. "Sports, Transgender Rights, and the Bodily Politics of Cisgender Supremacy." *Laws* 10, no. 3: 63. https://doi.org/10.3390/laws10030063.

Shuster, Stef. 2021. *Trans Medicine: The Emergence and Practice of Treating Gender*. New York: New York University Press.

Spade, Dean. 2008. "Documenting Gender." *Hastings Law Journal* 59, no. 1: 731–842.

Spade, Dean. 2011. *Normal Life: Administrative Violence, Critical Trans Politics, and the Limits of Law*. Cambridge, MA: South End.

Stanley, Eric. 2021. *Atmospheres of Violence: Structuring Antagonism and the Trans/Queer Ungovernable*. Durham, NC: Duke University Press.

Staurowsky, Ellen, Courtney Flowers, Erin Buzuvis, Lindsey Darvin, and Natalie Welch. 2022. "Fifty Years of Title IX: We're Not Done Yet." East Longmeadow, MA: Women's Sports Foundation.

Taylor, Jami K., Daniel C. Lewis, and Donald P. Haider-Markel. 2018. *The Remarkable Rise of Transgender Rights*. Ann Arbor: University of Michigan Press.

Towler, Christopher C., Nyron N. Crawford, and Robert A. Bennett. 2020. "Shut Up and Play: Black Athletes, Protest Politics, and Black Political Action." *Perspectives on Politics* 18, no. 1: 111–27.

Travers. 2009. "The Sport Nexus and Gender Injustice." *Studies in Social Justice* 2, no. 1: 79–101.

Travers. 2011. "Women's Ski Jumping, the 2010 Olympic Games, and the Deafening Silence of Sex Segregation, Whiteness, and Wealth." *Journal of Sport and Social Issues* 35, no. 2: 126–45.

Travers. 2014. "Sports." *TSQ* 1, nos. 1–2: 194–96.

Travers. 2016. "Transgender and Gender-Nonconforming Kids and the Binary Requirements of Sport Participation in North America." In *Child's Play: Sport in Kids' Worlds*, edited by Michael A. Messner and Michela Musto, 179–201. New Brunswick, NJ: Rutgers University Press.

US DOE (US Department of Education). 2021. "US Department of Education Confirms Title IX Protects Students from Discrimination Based on Sexual Orientation and Gender Identity." June 16. https://www.ed.gov/news/press-releases/us-department-education-confirms-title -ix-protects-students-discrimination-based-sexual-orientation-and-gender-identity.

US DOE (US Department of Education). 2023. "Fact Sheet: US Department of Education's Proposed Change to Its Title IX Regulations on Students' Eligibility for Athletic Teams." April 6. https://www.ed.gov/news/press-releases/fact-sheet-us-department-educations -proposed-change-its-title-ix-regulations-students-eligibility-athletic-teams.

Vitulli, Elias. 2010. "A Defining Moment in Civil Rights History? The Employment Non-discrimination Act, Trans-inclusion, and Homonormativity." *Sexuality Research and Social Policy* 7: 155–67.

Ware, Susan. 2011. *Game, Set, Match: Billie Jean King and the Revolution in Women's Sports*. Chapel Hill: University of North Carolina Press.

Williams, Juliet A. 2016. *The Separation Solution: Single-Sex Education and the New Politics of Gender Equality*. Oakland: University of California Press.

Woolley, Susan W. 2015. "'Boys Over Here, Girls Over There': A Critical Literacy of Binary Gender in Schools." *TSQ* 2, no. 3: 376–94.

Wuest, Joanna. 2019. "The Scientific Gaze in American Transgender Politics: Contesting the Meanings of Sex, Gender, and Gender Identity in the Bathroom Rights Cases." *Politics and Gender* 15, no. 2: 336–60.

Wuest, Joanna. 2021. "A Conservative Right to Privacy: Legal, Ideological, and Coalitional Transformations in US Social Conservatism." *Law and Social Inquiry* 46, no. 4: 964–92.

Zirin, Dave. 2009. *A People's History of Sports in the United States*. New York: New Press.

Creating a Non–Gender Binary Sports Space

The Nonbinary Policy of Korean "Queer Women Games"

JINSUN YANG

Abstract Trans inclusion policies remain one of the major issues facing contemporary trans rights movements in the United States. In sports, where sex segregation has rarely been challenged, trans inclusionary policies have emerged as a public debate in which key values of liberal individualism such as fairness, meritocracy, and safety collide with trans athletes' rights to belong in a public arena. While queer feminists' scholarship on sports has criticized the notion that trans inclusion policies do not necessarily problematize a binary gender ideology and sports institutions' authority in policing athletes' bodies, few studies have investigated alternative sports spaces and policies to challenge the sexist culture and binary sex-based structure of mainstream sports. This article introduces the Queer Women Games, a non–gender binary sports competition in Korea, as an experimental site to imagine and implement gender justice in sports through organizational actions and collective involvement. First, the author compares the QWG's nonbinary policies with transgender inclusion policies in recreational sports in terms of their approaches to sex segregation, sports authorities governing athletes' genders, and transgender exclusion. Then the author argues that the nonbinary policy opened a dialogue, which seems to be foreclosed in inclusion-based approaches, by undoing sex segregation and building a consensus on rejecting gender policing.

Keywords nonbinary policy, transgender, inclusion, recreational sports, organization

Queer Women Games is held annually since 2018 to create a sports culture resisting discrimination based on gender identity and sexual orientation in sports. Queer Women Games is a space where sex/gender/sexuality[1] minority women who have been excluded from sports reclaim their ground and enjoy sports with freedom and equal rights, and a space to advocate for human rights and sex/gender/sexuality equity. Queer Women Games is committed to sex/gender/sexuality diversity. The binary sex segregation of mainstream sports is not applicable to any match. Participants are not restricted by their sex/gender/sexuality identity, provided they are in agreement with the QWG's goals. Come and play at the Queer Women Games!

—2018 Queer Women Games Statement

TSQ: Transgender Studies Quarterly * Volume 10, Number 2 * May 2023

DOI 10.1215/23289252-10440762   © 2023 Duke University Press

O n June 17, 2018, the first Queer Women Games (QWG) was held by a Korean
queer activist group, Queer Women Network (QWN), at the Eunpyeong
District Sports Center in Seoul, South Korea. With its slogan "The Game Has
Already Begun," QWN proclaimed that the Korean government could not stop
queer/women[2] from taking part in sports competitions and taking over public
sports spaces. In Korea it was the first sports event highlighting the existence of
queer/women athletes. The QWG offered four official team sports: badminton
doubles, three-on-three basketball, four-hundred-meter relay, and futsal, a fast-
paced and small-sided soccer. The first and second QWGs had approximately 320
and 400 participants, respectively.

The QWG was no different from numerous amateur sports competitions
in Korea in that amateur athletes gathered to play sports, but it did have one key
difference: non–gender binary policies (henceforth, nonbinary policies). As the
QWG's 2018 statement indicates, all athletes play games with and against all genders without two-tiered sex segregation. Furthermore, the QWG does not restrict
its eligibility based on the sex or gender of participants, and the only requirement
is that participants are in agreement with the QWG's aims. This unprecedented
nonbinary policy brings critical questions to light about how this policy emerged
and developed. How do nonbinary policies impact the experiences of and access to
sports for trans and nonbinary people as well as cisgender people?

In this article, I examine the nonbinary policies at the QWG, policies
I define as attempting to undo binary sex segregation and that build a collective
consensus against probing or doubting others' sex/gender/sexual identities. Drawing on interview and ethnographic data, I analyze how nonbinary policies are
designed by organizers and experienced by athletes and audience members.
I argue that the QWG's nonbinary policies resist the persistent belief in binary
gender ideology in sports and sports authorities' policing of bodies, especially those
of trans, intersex, and nonbinary people and women. These points demonstrate
how nonbinary policies are distinct from trans inclusion policies[3] and shed light
on a collective approach to contest structural discrimination against trans, intersex, and nonbinary people and women in sports. Comparing the QWG's nonbinary policies to trans inclusion policies of recreational sports largely found in
the global North, I show how nonbinary policies address the limitations of trans
inclusion policies. To begin, I categorize current trans inclusion policies in recreational sports based on the conditions outlined in their clauses and demonstrate
their limits.

Trans Inclusion Policies in Recreational Sports

Studies of trans inclusion policies in sports have largely focused on those of elite
sports and physical education programs in schools. The former primarily concerns

Table 1. Trans inclusion policies in recreational sports

Restricted inclusion	Unrestricted inclusion
1. Requiring documentation and evidence	3. Inclusion based on self-identification
2. Inclusion conditions are unclear	4. Limiting cisgender males' access

I have collected fourteen trans inclusion policies in total. I took the latest version of many of them since they are continually updated. Trends show a transition from restricted inclusion to unrestricted inclusion. I categorized these documents in the following ways: (1) requiring documentation and evidence (n = 2): Ontario Soccer (Canada), Western States Endurance Run (US); (2) inclusion conditions are unclear (n = 3): Volleyball Canada, Wheelchair Basketball Canada, Cycling New Zealand; (3) inclusion based on self-identification (n = 7): International Quidditch Association, Big Apple Softball (US), Front Runners NY (US), Knickerbocker Sailing Association (US), Players Sport & Social Group (US), Whitehorse Women's Hockey League (Canada), International Gay and Lesbian Football Association; and (4) limiting the access of cisgender males (n = 2): Out to Swim (UK), US LGBT Soccer. Ontario Soccer is a provincial sports organization for soccer in Canada, promoting provincial, regional, school, and professional leagues. It is not typically an amateur sports organization, but I include it here as its structure reflects the inevitable overlap between amateur, recreational, and professional sports policies.

the policies of international sports organizations, including the International Olympic Committee (IOC) and the National Collegiate Athletic Association in the United States, while the latter concerns the policies of K–12 programs. Despite the scale and importance of recreational sports—since most people who are not professional athletes experience sports as a recreational activity—relatively little scholarly attention has been paid to trans inclusion policies in recreational sports. In part, this is because the policies of recreational sports organizations are not as well published or established as those of elite and educational sports organizations. Recreational sports, however, need to be illuminated as a space with greater practical potential for creating policies and practices to address sexist sports culture rooted in binary gender ideologies.[4] Drawing on data collected from transathlete .com,[5] I organize trans inclusion policies within recreational sports into four categories. First, the policies are categorized by whether they restrict inclusion, then by the details of their restrictions.

The first type of policy, restricted inclusion, requires documents related to one's transition—including medical or legal documents—for trans athletes to participate in the sports. Often, the required medical evidence is hormone treatment for at least one year prior to the race (WSER 2023).[6] Medical treatment requirements are largely limited to MTF athletes in the female leagues and are not often imposed on FTM athletes in the male leagues. Guidelines for restricted inclusion are mostly outlined by international governing bodies such as the IOC and World Athletics. Other than medical or legal evidence, it requires "documentation or evidence that shows the stated gender is sincerely held, and part of a person's core identity" (Ontario Soccer 2021: 30). The emphasis on sincerity and authenticity of (trans) athlete's gender identity align with two assumptions of sex testing in elite sports (Pieper 2016): first, cisgender athletes always sincerely preserve a binary gender as part of their core identity. Second, institutional sports could and should scrutinize and exclude those who may not sincerely hold one of the binary genders as their core identity, such as trans, intersex, and non-binary people or exceptional female athletes to preserve the "integrity of female athletics."[7]

The second type of policy is restricted inclusion with unclear conditions in policies (Ontario Soccer 2021; Cycling New Zealand 2020). For example, "Trans People Policy" from Cycling New Zealand (2020) states, "Cycling New Zealand and its members should treat a Trans person as belonging to the sex in which they present (as opposed to the biological sex they were born with) unless this is deemed to give the Trans person an unfair advantage, or would be a risk to the safety of competitors." The policy does not clarify what could be seen as "an unfair advantage" or "a risk to the safety of competitors." Considering that recreational and amateur sports tend to value having fun and building friendships in a community more than elite sports, the restricted inclusion implies that such policies prioritize fairness and safety for cisgender athletes over trans athletes. Overall, restricted inclusion involves proving the transition process to cisgender people. Contingent clauses can signify to trans people that this space is not inclusive of trans identity or may leave trans people vulnerable to discrimination (Pecoraro and Pitts 2020).

The third type of policy includes trans people without restrictions based on self-identification. For instance, Whitehorse Women's Hockey Association (2014) "welcomes any player who was born or identifies as a woman" The International Gay and Lesbian Football Association states, "A participant should take part in the IGLFA event in the gender of competition they feel reflects their identity best, which may be the gender that aligns with the sex they were assigned at birth or a different gender" (IGLFA 2021). Trans inclusion policies without restrictions are largely founded in the LGBTQ sports community and are often revisions of previous restricted policies.[8]

Lastly, there are policies that include trans people without restriction while limiting cisgender males' access in women leagues. Otherwise, all genders can participate in women/men's or mixed leagues. The "Transgender Inclusion Policy" of US LGBT Soccer (2019) reports, "Any person may play in a match involving men. Therefore, there are no conditions regarding an individual playing in a match under their reassigned/affirmed gender when participating in play designated for men, or men and women (coed). Males, unless identified as Transgender male, are not permitted to play in the female designated to play." The UK Out to Swim's (2020) "Diversity and Inclusion" explains that the "OTS welcomes all genders and has daily mixed-gender sessions. Recognizing the disparity in the proportion of male swimmers to female swimmers in the swimming discipline, there is also a dedicated women-only swim session at the Oasis Sports Centre on a

Table 2. Differences in approaches: Trans inclusion policy vs. nonbinary policy

	Trans inclusion policy	Nonbinary policy
Sex segregation	Conforming	Undoing
Sports authority governing athletes' genders	Maintaining	Rejecting
Transgender exclusion	Individualist: highlighting trans individuals and their bodies	Collectivist: highlighting organizational actions and collective involvement

I want to note that the QWG is a unique competition held by the QWN, a queer/feminist activist group in South Korea. The context of the QWG's policies is distinct from that of the trans inclusion policies in North American sport. Since the nonbinary policy was not specifically designed to include trans people in sports, it does not necessarily include more trans people in sports, although it explicitly challenges structural trans exclusion. Additionally, the QWG is an annual competition, which is very different from a sports community that is based on a strong membership, like a sports club. A more extensive examination would be needed to better determine how insights from the QWG apply to other types of sports communities.

Thursday evening." Although the policy is limited to sessions, not competition, it clarifies that the gender disparity resulting from cisgender male-dominant sports is the reason they restrict cisgender males' access to women's sessions. This strategy is in line with feminist scholarship's recommendation for "gender justice" (McDonagh and Pappano 2009; Travers 2009) in sports: coercive sex segregation needs to be eliminated while maintaining voluntary segregation to promote women's participation (McDonagh and Pappano 2009; Travers 2009).

Here I divided trans inclusion policies in recreational sports into four categories. Despite the differences between definitions and interpretations of inclusion, I argue that trans inclusion policies share several limitations in their inclusion-based approaches. Furthermore, a nonbinary policy approach opens dialogue, which is largely foreclosed in inclusion-based approaches.

The first limitation of transgender inclusion policies is that they follow binary sex segregation and therefore do not necessarily question the necessity of a two-tiered sex system. The persistent belief in the "advantage thesis" (Cavanagh and Sykes 2006), that those assigned males at birth have an unfair competitive advantage over those assigned females at birth, often remains intact in trans inclusion policies. Nonbinary people, including intersex and nonbinary trans people, are still excluded under transgender inclusion policies. On the other hand, a nonbinary policy fundamentally questions the necessity of sex segregation and challenges its underlying ideas.

Second, transgender inclusion policies maintain the authority of sports institutions over athletes' genders. In sanctioned events with trans inclusion policies, it is exclusively up to the sports organizations to decide which bodies are included in sports, that is, which bodies are eligible to implement moral values in modern sports such as fairness, integrity, and comradeship as well as competitiveness and strenuosity (Gems, Borish, and Pfister 2017). Restricted inclusion policies, especially through the proving process, reinforce hierarchical power relationships between athletes and sports authorities in policing bodies (Sullivan 2011). Even under transgender inclusion policies based on self-identification, athletes are required to identify their gender identity, which should align with binary gender in most cases, to sports organizations no matter what sports games or levels the athletes participate in. A nonbinary policy, by contrast, aims to build consensus against gender policing by individuals or sports organizations.

Third, inclusion-based policies take an individualistic approach to addressing the exclusion of trans people in two-sex tiered sports.[9] Here unrestricted inclusion policies are separated from restricted inclusion policies because the former acknowledges that the binary sex system excludes trans people and aims to reform the mainstream sports culture, while the latter demands that individual athletes prove their eligibility. In recreational sports, when taking the individual approach to trans inclusion, cisgender individuals accept trans individuals, a sex/gender minority, who want to be included in a sports community but cannot belong to women's or men's leagues. In this narrative, trans individuals should be recognized as transgender by non-trans individuals, which means that, to be included, they must come out first and advocate for their rights. Under such individualist approaches, it is still trans individuals who take on the burden problematizing trans exclusion in sports and justifying the value of trans inclusion policies. If a community has little awareness of trans people or does not have a trans member who came out, it becomes hard to argue for the necessity of a trans inclusion policy in the community. For example, Korean sports history has no record of trans athletes coming out in public, and there is a relatively low level of public awareness about trans people in sports. Additionally, threats of gender violence and discrimination prevent trans and nonbinary people from coming out while participating in sports. Because of these circumstances, it is very challenging to propose or set up a trans inclusion policy even in gay and lesbian sports communities. To circumvent these obstacles, the QWG created a nonbinary policy that takes a collectivist approach, foregrounding organizational actions and collective involvement in the fight against transgender exclusion and binary gender ideology in sports.

QWG: Organizational Strategies of Non–Gender Binary Policy

I conducted fieldwork in South Korea during the 2018–19 cycles of the QWG and used a variety of methods to gather empirical data on the games, including participant observations, interviews, and discourse analysis of visual and print media. Combining these methods allowed me to capture discourses and tensions surrounding the QWG from the perspectives of organizers and participants as well as to understand the experience and processes of the QWG. In total, I draw from

30 formal in-depth interviews, with a mix of organizers (n = 4), staff (n = 6), and athletes (n = 20). Athlete interviewees participated in four sports: relay (n = 8), futsal (n = 4), basketball (n = 4), and badminton (n = 2). I conducted all interviews in Korean and translated select interview quotes and excerpts from documents into English. All interviewee names have been changed to Korean first names that do not imply their sex/gender identity. Because all interviewees were participants in the QWG, which explicitly challenged the gender binary in sports, I adopt an alternative single pronoun, *they/them/theirs*, for all interviewees.[10]

The next section addresses nonbinary policies, a term I use to describe the following policies at the QWG. First, the QWG cancels the two-tiered sex system in sports by deleting the gender category in an entry form. The QWG athletes do not describe or disclose any information about their gender to any agents including the QWG organization, teammates, and competitors. Second, all participants agree to the oath of the QWG, which states they will not question or probe the sex/gender/sexuality identities of others. I examine the process by which these two policies were designed and implemented by organizers and experienced by participants and find that nonbinary policies are meant to confront binary gender ideology in sports at the interactional and organizational levels. Although I underline the role of organizational actions to challenge the legitimated gender policing in mainstream sports, I also find that building consensus on a nonbinary sports space among participants, including athletes, the audience, referees, and staff, is a key step in carrying out the nonbinary policies.

Strategy 1: Undoing Sex Segregation

Binary gender categories in sports demand that athletes conform to the two sex system and state their identities to determine eligibility (Sullivan 2011). Marking a gender category in entry forms may appear to athletes as a natural and non-negotiable process, no matter what types and levels of a sport they belong to, from K–12 sports to leisure sports to professional leagues. As a first step in undoing sex segregation, the QWG removed a gender marker from its entry forms. When asked about undoing sex segregation in the QWG, an organizer, Han, viewed the QWG as an "opportunity" to explore the relation between sex segregation and fairness.

> In sports, there are very deeply rooted ideas about physical difference. Because the person is a man, because the body is masculine, probably has a good athletic sense and would play better . . . people say "that is why this is unfair." It's a common idea that male and female bodies should be segregated for fairness. Fairness is such a pivotal value in sports, however, we did not really have a chance to discuss it. If sex segregation is necessary in sports, then what fairness would be found without

sex segregation? QWG brought the participants into this discussion. I thought it would be a great opportunity if we could learn and feel it together without sex segregation.

Han explained that the QWG's nonbinary policy was meant to open a discussion about the relationship between physical differences, sex segregation, and fairness, rather than dismissing the topic altogether. The undoing of sex segregation was designed to question the persistent belief in the necessity of sex segregation and explore what fairness would be found in the absence of a concept of fairness rooted in biological essentialism. In support of those goals, athletes face, contact, and compete against/with different bodies and are asked how they experience sex differences in the QWG and if the sex differences are the most salient factor to decide fairness in recreational and amateur sports.

As the QWG's statement highlights, undoing sex segregation is also to problematize discrimination against trans, intersex, and nonbinary people and women in the two-tiered sex system. From the perspective of those marginalized from mainstream sports, nonbinary policies fundamentally question who belongs and who is welcome in sports. In this sense, gender-neutral restrooms played a symbolic role in the QWG. Gender inclusive facilities are considered a crucial part of an environment in which all athletes are safe and treated fairly (Griffin and Carroll 2010). Joo, a futsal player, described their surprise and pleasure to have gender-neutral restrooms in the QWG: "The most surprising thing was gender-neutral restrooms. That was amazing. I remember the moment I changed my uniform there. It reminded me that I didn't have to categorize myself into man or woman. While changing the uniform, I felt very safe there." Athletes often changed their uniforms in the restroom, since a changing room was not offered on the site. Joo, who identified as genderqueer, found safety and freedom from compulsory binary categorization in the nonbinary restroom. When asked to describe more about the safety they felt, Joo explained the gender-neutral restroom reflected the fact that it was "full of people like me." Joo did not have any information about other participants' identities, like everyone else. What Joo underlined was their trust in, and bonds with, the QWG's participants, rather than the importance of sharing the same identity. For Joo, the gender-neutral restroom symbolized the QWG's commitment to gender equity over binary gender, which gave Joo a sense of belonging and safety. Joe's experience raises questions about the relationships between fairness, safety, and belonging in sports: When fairness is determined by the perspective of cisgender people, how can those who do not belong to a binary gender system or who do not feel safe in two-tiered sports argue for "level playing fields"? Is it possible to separate fairness from safety and a sense of belonging? The nonbinary policy complicates fairness by shedding light on unspoken assumptions and inextricably intertwined values.

Tensions and Discoveries across Sex Differences. When asked about nonbinary policies, the majority of interviewees emphasized their confusion and embarrassment at the beginning of the QWG. For example, a relay team complained to organizers about fairness at the site. Ahn, an organizer, responded to the complaint:

> Representatives of each relay team gathered to decide the order of the match. There was a group of men there. I mean a male presenting team. One female participant came to ask me, "Why do men participate in the game?" So, I explained the QWG's aims. We try to create a sports space everyone can enjoy over the gender binary. But she refuted me. She thought it was unfair. Women and men have different physiques then how come we compete against each other? At the planning stage, organizers had predicted and pondered this situation. It is one of the QWG's goals that we do not agree with the belief in the male body's superiority. Later, in the relay game, the gay[11] team was terribly defeated, and the team that raised the issue was ranked second. Then the complaint was totally gone.

While this was the only case in which a participant called into question undoing sex segregation at the site, another interviewee also mentioned that they looked up the QWG policies when they found "mixed-gender" presenting matches. Ahn's response to the complaints, reconfirming the goals and policies of the QWG, illustrates how important the building of consensus is to the creation of a nonbinary sports space. It was not surprising that some participants had concerns and complaints about nonbinary policies, since a nonbinary sports space was unprecedented to almost all participants, including organizers, and since most participants had prior experiences of exclusion and discrimination in cis-male dominant sports culture. Indeed, feminist scholars have underlined that, if undoing sex segregation is not accompanied by a fundamental challenge to sexist sports culture, women and LGBTQ people are likely to face an increased burden of sexism and misogyny (Travers 2013; Channon et al. 2016). Organizational actions (Cunningham 2015; Pape 2020), structural mechanisms (Musto 2014), and instructors and practitioners (Channon 2014) are needed at the interactional and organizational level to foster sex/gender/sexuality equity in sex-integrated sports. For the QWG, it was critical that participants question biological essentialism, the two-tiered sex system, and cis-male centered sports culture, so that participants would be open to undoing sex segregation in games. Under these goals, athletes played games without sex segregation, and all participants witnessed some games in which female presenting teams beat male presenting teams. After watching the matches, Shin, a relay athlete, admitted that they recognized the importance of skill over sex differences: "Honestly, it doesn't make sense. I'm 156 centimeters [5.1 feet] and what is the average height of the gay team? Some people were complaining 'How do lesbians compete with gays?' But when the game started, it turned out that was not really a thing but the gap between the elites and amateurs." Recreational sports, like the QWG, have a wide variation in athletes' athletic experience and skill level. Like Shin, who emphasized the gap between "elites and amateurs," other interviewees similarly reported that they discovered many determinants of athletic prowess other than sex: experience, passion, teamwork, resources, a sense of belonging and support. Although most interviewees admitted that the belief in the male body's superiority over the female body was not realized in the QWG, it does not mean the belief was completely debunked through the QWG experience. Still, once athletes found factors other than sex difference that determined athletic prowess, they believed, "We could beat them," as Joo, a futsal player, describes, "This is such a bias, but when we looked over the appearance of the Lion FC, we questioned 'Are they any good?' It might be a prejudice against gay if there were gays. But my team said 'We could beat them, we would win' (Laughs). They didn't look muscular or give off the macho men's aura. I thought it might be worth competing with them, but fortunately, we didn't have a match with them." Joo, a futsal player, described what happened in their team when they saw the Lion FC, a male presenting team in futsal games. They guessed Lion FC was a gay team because the team presented male although, they were not sure. Joo's team did not see Lion FC as a skilled team because they were not muscular. Joo said that "it was a prejudice against gay men," but they were guessing Lion FC was a gay team because they were a male presenting team, and their low expectations about the Lion FC's performance was deduced from their impression of the team's musculature. For Joo, the key point was not whether Lion FC were gay or not but how fit they were and how skilled they were as a competitor. Joo said it was "fortunate" not to compete with Lion FC, but they also hoped to have a chance to play against them. These findings demonstrate that when sex differences were blurred, athletes and audiences discovered differences within one sex category and more overlapping components across gender. As a result, the QWG shows that, when detached from biological essentialism, sports can illuminate a continuum of bodies and performances beyond the binary (Kane 1995).

Strategy 2: Rejecting Gender Policing

The QWG's second plan to create a nonbinary sports space was to build consensus on its policies that reject gender policing. The QWG has an oath called "Our Promises," a fundamental agreement among all participants not to doubt or probe other participants' sex/gender/sexuality identity. It was proclaimed at the opening ceremony by a delegation of athletes and organizers. Throughout the game season, the oath was also shared online on the QWG website, Twitter, and Facebook and printed on the participant pamphlet. The oath serves a crucial role in building consensus among participants, since not only organizations but also athletes and audience members often scrutinize and question athletes' bodies, gender, and eligibility in sports.

Our Promises

As we have come together to take part in the 2018 Queer Women Games,

1.   All participants are equal regardless of types of participation and are subjects who advocate gender equity and the human rights of sex/gender/sexuality minorities.

2.   Recognize that one's identity is best understood by themselves, and do not doubt or judge others' identities.

3.   Do not judge or act on stereotypes with respect to age, sex, sexual orientation, and gender identity of others.

4.   Keep in mind that the intimacy of physical contact varies from person to person and that the contact I want may be uncomfortable to others.

5.   Do not use an expression or label which disparages minorities (disability/women/age/race).

6.   If there is something you do not understand or feel uncomfortable about, actively express it, communicate it with others, and respond to it together.

7.   We promise mutual trust to create a safe and pleasant space for everyone. (my translation)

Clauses 2 and 3 specifically problematize sports authorities' governing and policing of bodies within the framework of the gender binary. Additionally, the promise not to judge another's sex/gender/sexuality means that nobody needs to identify themselves as a man, woman, or any other gender. Clause 2, "one's identity is best understood by themselves," privileges self-definition over medical-legal authority. Analyzing approaches to the gender binary, Travers (2006) distinguishes gender-conforming elements from gender-transforming elements in the transgender liberation movement. While trans inclusion policies take a gender-conforming strategy by challenging the biological and fixed assignment of people to male and female categories, nonbinary policies take a gender transforming strategy by questioning the binary category itself.

As all participants did not indicate their gender identity on the entry forms, QWN, the organization that holds the QWG, also did not collect any information about the participants' sex or gender identity. Because the QWG remained invested in the self-identities of participants rather than engaging in forms of institutional policing, participants' collective involvement was necessary to accomplish its goals. In that regard, clauses 6 and 7 addressed crucial and substantial consensus by stressing active engagement and mutual trust among participants.

Uncertain Others and Certain Ties.   The promise to not judge or probe others' sex/gender/sexuality identity required participants to remain uncertain about others. Still, the QWG participants read, misread, and responded to others' identities through socially constructed gender codes, as they do in everyday interaction. To deal with this unfamiliar state, participants used all their senses, tapped into a variety of knowledge, or withheld doing "gender attribution" (Kessler and McKenna 1985) or "determining gender" (Westbrook and Schilt 2014) of others. Kim, a relay runner who identified as genderqueer, connected the QWG's atmosphere to "a sense of liberation": "What most impressed me in QWG was that everyone was wearing sportswear and gym clothes, sweating, and sitting comfortably, regardless of their gender. Most people were women and queer and we felt each other. It definitely gave me a sense of liberation. Even though I don't make a good outcome in matches, I don't have to worry about the perception that this is because I'm a woman." Kim's description of the QWG illustrated how the promises of rejecting gender policing affected the sporting culture in the QWG and built ties among participants. Under "our promises," athletes could distance themselves from the self-censorship of mainstream sports—if I look feminine or masculine enough not to be suspected. Because of "a sense of liberation," Kim revealed, "I could be serious on games," and "I enjoyed the process in which I could do my best with my team."

Other interviewees also reported that they were not exposed to the same stresses and sexual harassment that they had in mainstream sports spaces. Therefore, they could focus more on games and enjoy themselves. For example, Jo, a relay runner who identified as genderqueer, foregrounded the role of the "promise" in the QWG: "Still, in QWG, some people might think in the same way. Hey, how come I run with that guy? But at least there was a promise not to talk about it. So, nobody brought me the doubt and I could enjoy the games." Choi, who participated in the relay, was an amateur basketball athlete for over ten years and reported countless negative experiences with male athletes.[12] For example, they noted, "I don't think people who come to QWG will regard me as an object of sexual harassment or do not give me an equal opportunity since they see me as a woman. That's probably a matter of value." Choi summarized their previous experience with male athletes by highlighting two emotions. One was that they were "scared of bumping into each other and getting hurt," and another was feeling "annoyed because they don't give me a ball." However, Choi welcomed the nonbinary policy of the QWG and noted their reason: "It would be different because I believe the participants will respect me as an equal competitor." When asked how the QWG differed from other amateur competitions, Choi emphasized friendship and a sense of belonging: "The friendly atmosphere in the match made a difference. This was only a temporary gathering, and I don't even know who you are, yet we are here together to create and enjoy this new trial named Queer Women Games. . . . Such friendly feelings. I came not just to play, but also to enjoy the event itself." Choi underlined their experience as an audience member as well as a player. While Choi displayed stronger bonds in the QWG than other interviewees, most noted a friendly atmosphere and a sense of belonging.

Kim, Jo, and Choi revealed the distinct difficulties they had to deal with in the mainstream sports culture: the self-censorship, transphobia, and sexual harassment against women. The collective promises against gender policing and sexual harassment gave these athletes trust that they did not need to worry about questioning their gender identity, eligibility, and safety. Participants' mutual trust was not built through the transparent sharing of their identities, but through promises not to probe each other's identities and the acceptance of uncertainty. Above all, these certain ties, and trust in the QWG, gave them an opportunity to enjoy the games without the concerns about gender policing and sexual harassment.

On the ground, the QWG participants had to work to actively combat assumptions steeped in the gender binary. While there was some initial resistance to the nonbinary policies set out by the organization, athletes were quickly socialized into the expectations of the QWG and learned to question underlying ideas about fairness, sex difference, and gender presentation. Alongside these challenges, participants like Kim, Jo, and Choi experienced moments of recognition, solidarity, and trust in the nonbinary sports world of the QWG. That is, in the QWG, the identities of nonbinary athletes were acknowledged and were not a barrier to entry. This stands in contrast to sports leagues with restrictive trans inclusionary policies, which rely on the binary to adjudicate participation. Moreover, the QWG dealt head-on with participants' sexist experiences of being harassed, questioned, and belittled in mainstream sporting events.

Conclusion

This article focuses on sets of organizational strategies and collective practices that constructed a nonbinary sports competition, the QWG. By comparing nonbinary policies to inclusion-based policies, I argue that the QWG's nonbinary policies opened a dialogue that seems foreclosed in an inclusion-based approach: a dialogue about the necessity of sex segregation, sports authorities' practice of governing bodies, and the discriminatory effects of individualistic approaches to transgender exclusion. By undoing sex segregation and refusing gender policing in sports, the nonbinary policies questioned the assumptions of a two-tiered sex system, binary sex essentialism, and the superiority of the male body. Consensus among participants and collective involvement were crucial to the success of two organizational actions. Once the discourse around binary sex difference was blurred in the QWG, participants discovered diverse factors other than sex difference that decide fairness and athletic prowess: skill, experience, passion, teamwork, resources, and a sense of belonging and support. While preserving the uncertainty of others, the promises not to police gender allowed participants to enjoy the games without the self-censorship, transphobia, and sexual harassment they had to deal with in mainstream sports.

In focusing on the organizational strategies and collective involvement of participants, this article illuminates a collectivistic approach to transgender exclusion in sports that tends to be ignored in inclusion-based approaches. The QWG's experiment to create a nonbinary sports space helps us imagine and explore alternative approaches to promote gender justice in sports at the interactional and organizational level.

Jinsun Yang is a graduate student in the sociology program at the University of Oregon. They teach and learn about transnational feminism, sex segregation in public spaces, and LGBTQ movements. They are a queer feminist activist in South Korea and an organizer of the Korean Queer Women Games.

Acknowledgments

I would like to thank the Queer Women Network and the interviewees for their trust and support in this research. I would also like to thank Johyeon Bang, Oluwakemi M. Balogun, Ryan Light, Jill Ann Harrison, and Justin Szasz for their helpful guidance and suggestions. Lastly, I wish to acknowledge the outstanding insights from the guest editors, CJ Jones and Travers, and three anonymous reviewers from *TSQ*. This research was supported by a research grant from the Center for the Study of Women in Society at the University of Oregon.

Notes

1. The Korean term 성 (性, *seong*) encompasses the categories of sex, gender, and sexuality identity in English, although *sex* (섹스), *gender* (젠더), and *sexuality* (섹슈얼리티) are adopted loanwords in Korea. In this article, I interpret 성 (性, *seong*) as *sex/gender/sexuality* in English.

2. *Queer/women* is a term introduced by the QWG organizers. They use queer/women both as a category and slogan. As a category, queer/women encompasses queer people, women, and those who cannot be divided into either category.

3. Trans inclusion policies are sometimes called transgender inclusion policies, gender inclusion policies, or inclusion policies. They are also sometimes included as untitled guidelines. In this article, I refer to them as trans inclusion policies.

4. I do not mean that recreational and amateur sports place less value on fairness, competition, or maintaining records. Rather, I want to highlight that recreational and amateur sports tend to develop their own cultures and practices relatively independently of the guidelines of legal and educational authorities.

5. This website gathers and provides information concerning trans inclusive policies and practices in athletics at various levels.

6. "Transgender women can register to compete: in the female category provided they have been undergoing continuous, medically supervised hormone treatment for gender transition for at least one year prior to the race, or in the male category with no restrictions.

Transgender men can register to compete: in the male or female category, unless they are undergoing hormone treatment related to gender transition that includes testosterone or any other banned substance in which case they must register in the male category." (WSER 2023).

7.   In 2019, when the Court of Arbitration for Sport ruled against Caster Semenya's eligibility in the Olympics, it announced that "such discrimination is a necessary, reasonable and proportionate means of achieving the IAAF's aim of preserving the integrity of female athletics in the Restricted Events" (Busch 2021).

8.   The current gender inclusion policy of the IGLFA was revised from the restricted inclusion policy in 2014, which stated, "The IGLFA must receive sufficient confirmation and be satisfied by documentation or evidence that shows the stated gender is sincerely held, and is part of a person's core identity" (IGLFA 2021).

9.   The individualist approach to trans inclusion has been dominantly constructed in two institutions: elite sports, especially Olympic sports, and laws such as Title IX (Sykes 2006). In the highly competitive elite sports world, individual athletes' bodies are formally and unquestionably scrutinized, displayed, and compared to each other, since the individual is considered the most significant and compelling unit even in team sports. However, the individual approach of restricted inclusion policies does not attend to experiences and values in recreational sports, in which athletes' skill levels substantially vary over the binary sex and athletes appreciate joy, friendship, and community as much as competition.

10.   While asking about pronouns is becoming a widespread practice in the West, it is not common in Korea. Therefore, I did not ask my interviewees their preferred pronoun. A single pronoun, *they/them/theirs*, is a known term that is mostly used by androgynous or nonbinary people in English-speaking North America. It is appreciated as a gender-inclusive linguistic change by LGBTQ+ communities, yet not accepted by all androgynous and nonbinary people. Nonbinaryness and androgyny are often represented by normative assumptions of whiteness, thinness, and masculinity, and *they/them/their* is also criticized as a white-centered phenomenon.

11.   Interviewees often used sexuality and gender interchangeably or sexuality as a shorthand for gender to make sense of others' identities. Here, I do not delve into the analysis for the purposes of this article.

12.   The QWG's policy does not allow athletes to participate in more than one sport.

References

Busch, Sven. 2021. "Caster Semenya Loses Testosterone Case against the IAAF in CAS Ruling." International Olympic Committee, February 10. https://olympics.com/en/news/caster -semenya-cas-testosterone-decision-iaaf.

Cavanagh, Sheila L., and Heather Sykes. 2006. "Transsexual Bodies at the Olympics: The International Olympic Committee's Policy on Transsexual Athletes at the 2004 Athens Summer Games." *Body and Society* 12, no. 3: 75–102. https://doi.org/10.1177/1357034X06067157.

Channon, Alex. 2014. "Towards the 'Undoing' of Gender in Mixed-Sex Martial Arts and Combat Sports." *Societies* 4, no. 4: 587–605. https://doi.org/10.3390/soc4040587.

Channon, Alex, Katherine Dashper, Thomas Fletcher, and Robert J. Lake. 2016. "The Promises and Pitfalls of Sex Integration in Sport and Physical Culture." *Sport in Society* 19, nos. 8–9: 1111–24. https://doi.org/10.1080/17430437.2016.1116167.

Cunningham, George B. 2015. "LGBT Inclusive Athletic Departments as Agents of Social Change." *Journal of Intercollegiate Sport* 8, no. 1: 43–56. https://doi.org/10.1123/jis.2014-0131.

Cycling New Zealand. 2020. "Trans People Policy." Updated February. https://www.cycling newzealand.nz/assets/CNZ/Resources/Organisation-Documents/Trans-Person-Policy -Updated-21-February-2020.pdf.

Gems, Gerald R., Linda J. Borish, and Gertrud Pfister. 2017. *Sports in American History: From Colonization to Globalization.* 2nd ed. Champaign, IL: Human Kinetics.

Griffin, Pat, and Helen J. Carroll. 2010. *On the Team: Equal Opportunity for Transgender Student Athletes.* National Center for Lesbian Rights, October 4. https://www.nclrights.org/wp -content/uploads/2013/07/TransgenderStudentAthleteReport.pdf.

IGLFA (International Gay and Lesbian Football Association). 2021. "IGLFA Gender Inclusion Policy." https://www.iglfa.org/wp-content/uploads/2021/03/IGLFA-GENDER-INCLUSION -POLICY-2021KH_.docx.pdf

Kane, Mary Jo. 1995. "Resistance/Transformation of the Oppositional Binary: Exposing Sport as a Continuum." *Journal of Sport and Social Issues* 19, no. 2: 191–218. https://doi.org/10.1177 /019372395019002006.

Kessler, Suzanne J., and Wendy McKenna. 1985. *Gender: An Ethnomethodological Approach.* Chicago: University of Chicago Press.

McDonagh, Eileen L., and Laura Pappano. 2009. *Playing with the Boys: Why Separate Is Not Equal in Sports.* New York: Oxford University Press.

Musto, Michela. 2014. "Athletes in the Pool, Girls and Boys on Deck: The Contextual Construction of Gender in Coed Youth Swimming." *Gender and Society* 28, no. 3: 359–80. https://doi .org/10.1177/0891243213515945.

Ontario Soccer. 2021. "2022 and 2023 Operational Procedures." Last updated December 4. https:// cdn1.sportngin.com/attachments/document/3f18-1747732/Ontario_Soccer_2022-2023 _Operational_Procedures.pdf.

Out to Swim. 2020. "Diversity and Inclusion at Out to Swim." https://www.outtoswim.org/edi (accessed April 20, 2022).

Pape, Madeleine. 2020. "Gender Segregation and Trajectories of Organizational Change: The Underrepresentation of Women in Sports Leadership." *Gender and Society* 34, no. 1: 81– 105. https://doi.org/10.1177/0891243219867914.

Pecoraro, Jennifer A., and Brenda G. Pitts. 2020. "Perceived Meanings and Implications of Transgender Inclusive Policies in Collegiate Recreation: An Exploratory Study." *Recreational Sports Journal* 44, no. 1: 67–75. https://doi.org/10.1177/1558866120909472.

Pieper, Lindsay Parks. 2016. *Sex Testing: Gender Policing in Women's Sports.* Sport and Society. Urbana: University of Illinois Press.

Sullivan, Claire F. 2011. "Gender Verification and Gender Policies in Elite Sport: Eligibility and 'Fair Play.'" *Journal of Sport and Social Issues* 35, no. 4: 400–419. https://doi.org/10.1177 /0193723511426293.

Sykes, Heather. 2006. "Transsexual and Transgender Policies in Sport." *Women in Sport and Physical Activity Journal* 15, no. 1: 3–13. https://doi.org/10.1123/wspaj.15.1.3.

Travers. 2006. "Queering Sport: Lesbian Softball Leagues and the Transgender Challenge." *International Review for the Sociology of Sport* 41, nos. 3–4: 431–46. https://doi.org/10.1177 /1012690207078070.

Travers. 2009. "The Sport Nexus and Gender Injustice." *Studies in Social Justice* 2, no. 1: 79–101. https://doi.org/10.26522/ssj.v2i1.969.

Travers. 2013. "Thinking the Unthinkable: Imagining an 'Un-American,' Girl-Friendly, Women- and Trans-Inclusive Alternative for Baseball." *Journal of Sport and Social Issues* 37, no. 1: 78–96. https://doi.org/10.1177/0193723512455926.

US LGBT Soccer. 2019. "Transgender Inclusion Policy." Updated January 2019. https://www.uslgbtsoccer.org/transgender-inclusive-policy/.

Westbrook, Laurel, and Kristen Schilt. 2014. "Doing Gender, Determining Gender: Transgender People, Gender Panics, and the Maintenance of the Sex/Gender/Sexuality System." *Gender and Society* 28, no. 1: 32–57. https://doi.org/10.1177/0891243213503203.

Whitehorse Women's Hockey Association. 2014. "Hello WWHA, As you may know we have a player who is in the news talking about his journey transitioning from female to male . . ." Facebook, December 19. https://www.facebook.com/whitehorsewomenshockeyassn/posts/772283902807785.

WSER (Western States Endurance Run). 2023. "Transgender and Nonbinary Entrant Policy." https://www.wser.org/transgender-entrant-policy/ (accessed March 13, 2023).

Close Encounters of the Anxious Kind

Notes on Transfeminine Exclusion from Sports and Dating

TRISTAN VENTURI

Abstract This essay considers the shared ideological foundation underlying transfeminine exclusion from sports and transfeminine exclusion from dating. While biological advantage and sexual preference are often cited as indisputable, legitimate, and scientifically supported criteria for prohibiting transgender participation in these two domains, the author argues that both sports and dating operate according to fallacious cisheteronormative assumptions that work to ostracize sex/gender-transgressive bodies through three main practices: the exercise of suspicion, the legitimization of inspection, and the criminalization of nondisclosure.

Keywords transgender women, transgender athletes, sports, dating, transgender exclusionary discourse

American mixed martial arts (MMA) fighter Fallon Fox had been training and competing in the women's division for five years when, in 2013, a phone call irreversibly altered the course of her career. Pressured by a journalist's allusions to her past, Fox revealed her previously undisclosed transgender identity, leading to controversy (Zeigler 2013). Ultimate Fighting Championship color commentator Joe Rogan has been among the most vocal media personalities in decrying the presence of transgender women athletes in all-female competition, particularly with respect to contact sports. In a 2018 YouTube video viewed over 5 million times, Rogan likened his spectatorial experience of hand-to-hand combat between Fox and her cisgender opponents to "watching a former man beat up women who never had the benefits of thirty years plus of testosterone in their body," and he adduced insurmountable biological differences between the sexes in support of his argument: "We're built different. It's just a fact. Anyone who tries to argue that is crazy." Rogan further complained that, while cisgender athletes should be allowed to deliberately fight transgender rivals if they wish to, Fox's failure to preemptively divulge her gender history was an aggravating factor that endangered "women who think they were fighting a woman and got fucking smashed" (JRE Clips 2018a).

TSQ: Transgender Studies Quarterly ∗ Volume 10, Number 2 ∗ May 2023 **133**
DOI 10.1215/23289252-10440776 © 2023 Duke University Press

A decade after Fox's coerced coming out, transgender identities are as visible as ever—and not solely among sports communities. As a trans man, I often wonder what this long-awaited, newly gained visibility is bound to entail for those who do not wish to become involved with "us" in any sphere of their existence, whether public or private. Last year, I came across a study by Richard Mocarski and colleagues (2019: 423) investigating the ambiguities of the "duality of exposure" produced by the recent rise in transgender visibility. "It's great that transitioning is coming to light," observed one trans participant who came oddly close to regretting the proverbial "tipping point." "The problem is all the flip side of it. . . . People are stalking people in the bathroom and the thing is trans people were going into the bathroom they were supposed to be going in and you didn't know until we made it a big deal and now it's a problem." To be sure, this is an oversimplified account that does little justice to the complexity of the subject. Still, I was surprised to realize how, until then, I had not given enough consideration to a simple yet crucial fact: greater visibility could be incentivizing gender surveillance at both individual and institutional levels. In other words, the more visible we are, the more entitled our society might feel to look for us. As the interviewee rightfully notes, this behavior is most likely to occur within sex-segregated shared spaces; public restrooms did feature prominently in the crossfire between supporters and detractors of trans rights legislation (Schilt and Westbrook 2015). Nevertheless, we know the fear of transgender infiltration to be a culturally pervasive phenomenon, resembling nothing short of a moral panic and affecting other realms perhaps less obtrusively, yet just as profoundly.

In my everyday experience, I have come to notice how two specific domains—sports and dating—are consistently cited as sui generis scenarios in which a moratorium on transgender inclusion ought to be applied, owing to factors that are often presented (and hastily accepted) as self-explanatory: biological differences and sexual preferences. I have had the disappointing chance to hear this argument time and again via mainstream media, among my own circle of otherwise supportive friends, and, strikingly, within the trans community itself. In fact, I have found that most acquaintances of mine who would rather not date trans folks or see them compete describe themselves as allies and do, as a matter of fact, genuinely advocate for inclusion in other contexts. Rogan himself inadvertently subscribed to this line of reasoning in another of his clips:

> I think it's ridiculous to have a trans woman compete against women in mixed martial arts. You wanna have a dude in chess? You wanna have a dude in something that's non-physical? Sure. You want them to be a woman? Yes, okay. You want them to be recognized as a woman? Sure. But as soon as you're compelling people. . . . Like, here's one that's been going up lately: if you don't want to date a trans woman, then you're some sort of a bigot. (JRE Clips 2018b)

This recurring and often unintended association had me wondering. Why sports? Why dating? Rogan's words gesture toward an ill-concealed fear of being "compelled" into "physical" proximity with transfeminine bodies. Could the overreliance on the alleged undeniability of biology and sexual taste be enshrouding deep-seated anxieties around coming into contact with transgender embodiment? Why the cultural recalcitrance to envision such "close encounters" as volitional, enthusiastic acts of intimacy void of any forcible component? This essay brings into conversation patterns of transgender exclusion from sports and patterns of transgender exclusion from dating, which I find to be eerily similar and worthy of critical attention. Drawing from existing literature on both realms, I expose the limitations of the biological difference and sexual preference theses through the identification and critique of three flagrantly political elements—suspicion, inspection, and deception—that subtend exclusionary dynamics. Ultimately, I argue that transgender bodies struggle to find acceptance in sports and dating, owing to a general inability to conceptualize meaningful scenarios of cis-trans bodily intimacy. In this sense, rather than exist as impenetrable strongholds operating under the indisputability of science, the worlds of sports and dating are undergirded by larger systems of oppression, in which (cis)sexist, (trans)misogynistic, and racist assumptions interlock to ostracize transgressive female bodies.

Transgender Women and Sports

Western sports culture has been recognized as a highly gendered site (Wackwitz 2003), in which essentialist conceptualizations of sex and gender are reinforced and perpetuated, along with sexism (Messner 1988), heterosexism (Griffin 1998), and masculine privileging (McDonagh and Pappano 2007). Notions of femininity and masculinity in sports are concurrently shaped by racist, nationalist, and imperialist discourse (Anderson and Travers 2017; Karkazis and Jordan-Young 2018; Travers 2018). The racialized, sex/gender-transgressive bodies of sportswomen from the global South (and, in the past, those from the Eastern Bloc) endure disproportionate levels of scrutiny, commentary, and spectacularization (Pastor 2019). Since transgender identity similarly negates the sex/gender binary and develops along racialized lines (Beauchamp 2019; Snorton 2017), trans athletes are increasingly subject to comparable modalities of hypersurveillance, owing to the radical ways in which they complicate gendered embodiment (Pilgrim, Martin, and Binder 2003; Anderson and Travers 2017). Increased trans visibility led to the promulgation of tailored eligibility regulations by the world's leading sports governing bodies. Among the side effects of such heightened cultural attention, however, was the revival of robust waves of gender panics around the presence of "sex impostors" in women's athletics (Anderson and Travers 2017). Regrettably, some radical feminist fringes have incorporated the debate into their rapidly spreading anti-trans propaganda, exploiting the "biological advantage" thesis to their own benefit. According to this most popular exclusionary argument, a trans sportswoman's history of male puberty would lend her a set of physical advantages over cisgender adversaries, thereby compromising fair play (Pearce, Erikainen, and Vincent 2020).

Despite there being no conclusive evidence in support of such claims (Jones et al. 2017), it nonetheless continues to dominate public opinion. Studies indicate that most Americans disapprove of transgender athletes competing according to their gender identity, whether at school or elite level (Bahrampour, Clement, and Guskin 2022; McCarthy 2021). Gender traditionalism and gender identity conformity were identified as reliable predictors of aversion to trans inclusion (Flores et al. 2020). A study by Jamie Cleland, Ellis Cashmore, and Kevin Dixon (2021) showed that a considerable number of sports fans believe that trans athletes are seeking an "easy win" by choosing to play as women in disciplines where they could not succeed as men, and that allowing them to do so is to prioritize political correctness over the safety of (cisgender) women. Participants called trans inclusion in sports "distorted and unfair" and described it as "the taking of male biological advantages over females and injecting it into the female sports arena" (9–10). Additionally, the 2021 National Sports Public Opinion Pulse Update found that 45 percent of respondents agreed with the statement, "I am concerned about the presence of transgender athletes' presence in the locker room"—an aspect that bespeaks a cultural investment in constructing transfeminine identity as an insidious reincarnation of male violence (Global Sport Institute 2021: 22). Concerns over fair play have also been endorsed by some cisgender athletes (Cavanagh and Sykes 2006). Worryingly, heated debates around trans sportswomen's alleged advantage and inbuilt "male" temper continue to influence not only media discourse (Cavanagh and Sykes 2006; Lucas and Newhall 2018) but also policy making (Sharrow 2021), with significant repercussions on the careers and lives of the individuals concerned.

Transgender Women and Dating

Research into the romantic lives of transgender individuals is appallingly scarce, predominantly clinical in nature, and focused on longtime couples (Buggs 2020). For the most part, transgender people's dating experiences remain uncharted territory. However, we do know that a "blanket ban" attitude returns here, in that most Americans purposely exclude trans folks from their dating pool (Blair and Hoskin 2019); again, gender traditionalism and gender identity conformity stand out as salient contributing factors (Anderson 2018). In fact, although we are used to conceiving of sexual and romantic attraction as purely instinctual, it is imperative to recognize that "mate selection is still frequently restricted by social values and prejudices" (Blair and Hoskin 2019: 2075) and that "tastes" are overall less spontaneous and inflexible than we tend to believe (Parker and Gagnon 1995; Rubin 2006). For instance, Jessica Mao, Mara Haupert, and Eliot Smith (2019: 820) found that "trans labels reliably reduce heterosexual perceivers' sexual and romantic attraction." Indeed, women report that disclosing their trans status often causes straight men to "reconsider" their initial interest (Iantaffi and Bockting 2011; Serano 2007). Individuals might filter out folks based on transgender status alone, despite the remarkable variety of phenotypic attributes found among trans bodies—including genital conformation and aesthetic appearance, which are commonsensically linked to attraction.

In what would appear as a paradox, high rates of romantic rejection correlate with sexual objectification. This is especially true of cisgender heterosexual males who disproportionately target Black and Brown trans women, once again leading to racialized, sex/gender-transgressive bodies carrying the heaviest stigma (Gamarel et al. 2022). The latest Human Rights Campaign report on anti-trans violence found a substantial overlap between misogynistic, transphobic, and racist hate across multiple areas, including intimate relationships (Human Rights Foundation 2021). Furthermore, male-to-female (MtF) transitions are often portrayed as driven by a desire for sexual intimacy with (otherwise unavailable) straight men, to the extent that trans women are occasionally presumed to provoke their own sexualization (Serano 2007). Unlike transmasculine folks, MtF persons are "culturally marked, not for failing to conform to gender norms per se, but because of the specific direction of their gender transgression" in a sexist world that glorifies masculinity while belittling femininity (Serano 2012). In "transmisogynoir" (Bailey and Trudy 2018), misogynistic and anti-Black prejudices and tropes (e.g., the "hypersexual" Black woman) meet transphobic stances. Further marginalized, these identities are eventually construed as undesirable in the long term and merely "good for sex" (Gamarel et al. 2022).

Suspicion

Last year, the poorly phrased headline of a local newspaper in Carrara, Italy, grabbed my attention: "Woman Hits Boyfriend with 'Suspect' Vigor and He Finds out She's Trans." According to the article, the woman's "shocking" display of strength turned out to be a reliable indicator of her previously unknown sex assigned at birth (Esposito 2022). The incident immediately reminded me of Gwen Araujo's tragic end. In 2002 seventeen-year-old Araujo was murdered in Newark, California, by four male acquaintances who had engaged in sex with her prior to discovering her transgender status. The nonconsensual inspection of her genitals was preceded by a progression of allegedly suspect signs, including the fact that she "fought like a guy" (Hanley and Garrison 2002). I then remembered a YouTube interview in which Ashlee Evans-Smith, a cisgender MMA athlete who defeated Fallon Fox in 2013, was asked whether Fox's strength felt any different compared to that of cisgender fighters. Evans-Smith admitted that "definitely, when her striking made impact on my face, I could feel I got rocked. She kind of hit harder than some of my guy teammates hit" (MMA Interviews 2013).

In a cissexist culture where "gender is assumed to be cisgender" (Ashley 2018: 344) and "transgender identity is in itself a provocation" (Barker-Plummer 2013: 715), the exercise of suspicion plays a rather instrumental role in discerning unruly bodies. As such, suspicion presupposes "a problematic adherence to binary and immutable bodily accounts of gender" (716). A girl's higher-than-average force is to be interpreted as a symptom of biological maleness, whereas a trans woman's athletic ability will automatically be classified as "male" regardless of actual performance. Araujo, like the woman who made headlines in Carrara, possessed "unfeminine" strength before the eyes of her dates; therefore, her womanhood had to be thrown into question—and rather violently so. Vice versa, Fox made her transgender identity known; therefore, her opponent was invited to dig for the fossils of a previous maleness. Tellingly, this process foregrounds the identification of "male" cues, like strength, as the primary path to "determining gender" (Westbrook and Schilt 2013) and to bolstering the myth of the frail, unthreatening female body as naturally incapable of sustaining the strain of sports performance (Dowling 2000). As Julia Serano (2007) points out, the stigmatization of transfemininity is less the result of transphobia than it is of sexism. In that respect, the suspicion of transfeminine bodies is very much about the policing of all women's bodies and the punishment of those who do not comply with the requirements of White, heteronormative femininity. Fox, a mixed-race trans combat athlete, was called a "lying, sick, sociopathic, disgusting freak" (Iole 2013)—a description that perfectly suits the "black feminine abjection" prototype (Carby quoted in Fischer and McClearen 2020: 155).

To base one's "gender suspicions" on aesthetic parameters or even performance metrics (e.g., strength, speed, endurance), however, is quite a losing proposition. Gender passing is an illuminating concept here. As Thomas Billard (2019: 465) writes, passing "challenges assumptions of physiological evidence in accurate social categorization, regardless of the direction in which the passing occurs." In simpler words, and ironically, transgender bodies can go undetected, while cisgender ones might not "pass." Gender critical activists who recently unleashed their exclusionary views on trans sportswomen via Twitter are a case in point. "Very male build. Maybe this individual should compete with the . . . males," said one Twitter user of *cisgender* swimmer Katie Ledecky (Reed 2022). Sierra Schmidt, also a cisgender swimmer, was erroneously read as trans and accused of "making fun of women, parodying exaggerated femininity" as she performed her extravagant warm-up dance (Fairchild 2022). An image of trans MMA fighter Alana McLaughlin and her cis adversary facing each other went viral after one outraged user pointed out that "the transgender is like six feet tall and completely towers over the normal woman." The original tweet was deleted once McLaughlin herself replied with a correction: "You know I'm the short one, right?" (Riaz 2021).

These and other hilarious gaffes are instructive in demonstrating how fallacious and misleading "appearance-based suspicions" (Pieper 2016b: 29) can be, as well as how they revolve around the presence of "masculine" attributes such as size and height. In actuality, these essentialist interpretations are resoundingly flawed (Fausto-Sterling 2000) and fail to recognize that "sexual development is a multistep process influenced by an assortment of genetic factors" (Pieper 2016b: 5). Research indicates that variations between the sexes are less pronounced than commonly believed; instead, "differences within a gender are much larger than the average differences between genders" (Ivy and Conrad 2018: 120). In sports, this is true of physiological traits such as height, bone density, and lean body mass, proving that "individual characteristics ultimately matter more than group characteristics" (McDonagh and Pappano 2007: 64). Still, selected female athletes are currently required to undergo "suspicion-based testing" (Pilgrim, Martin, and Binder 2003). Additionally, the focus on gendered appearance deflects from the racial undertones of gender profiling, as most targets of gender verification are sportswomen from the global South. In 2009, following her victory at the World Championship, South African middle-distance runner Caster Semenya became "one of the world's most scrutinized athletes." Semenya's perceived "unfemininity" triggered intense media speculations about her "real" sex, exemplifying how testing is "reserved for women perceived as not feminine enough. . . . Gender variance has always incited scrutiny, and this scrutiny is often racialized" (Karkazis 2016). Additionally, homophobic assumptions were also at work here, as the targeting of "hypermasculine" women like Semenya betrays a "fear of female masculinization as a signifier of nonheterosexuality" (Pieper 2016b: 101).

Suspicion promotes similar misconceptions within dating scenarios. As Karen L. Blair and Rhea Ashley Hoskin (2019: 2086) argue, "We know very little about what the average cisgender person knows or thinks of trans bodies." In my experience, it is plausible and even common to date someone without ever realizing or discovering their transness. Nevertheless, many obsess over being able to "tell." An outré WikiHow vade mecum titled "Trying to Figure Out if Your Date Is Trans?" has been coedited by ninety-eight authors, translated into eight languages, and viewed over 680,000 times at the time of writing. Its Q&A section gathers several anxious comments inquiring about "the kind of hair a transgender person would have" and other "physical characteristics that show if someone is transgender or not" (WikiHow 2022). Several Reddit users seem to share the same palpable investment in securing access to potential partners' gender histories and ruling out those that happen to include gender transition. Here, many lament the absence of "a 'show me trans women' option, deselected by default" that would spare them the "guesswork" (a_dolf_please 2021) and allow them to "weed [trans women] out from the normal, ACTUAL women" (PhriekModeUSA 2021). Male anxieties around the potential inability to identify a woman as transgender— or, conversely, recognize a cis woman as such—highlight the inefficacy of suspicion. They also suggest that, as Toby Beauchamp (2019: 11–12) contends, *transgender* should be read "not as a predetermined category into which identities and bodies are slotted, but as a category *produced* in part through practices of surveillance in Western modernity" (emphasis added). Suspicion actively produces *transgender*—and, at large, deviancy—by discerning between "docile" and "unruly" bodies based on limited, misleading, and ideologically clouded medico-scientific information (Fausto-Sterling 2000).

Inspection

Sex testing involves a set of medical assessments aimed at ascertaining whether a (female) athlete's anatomical or biochemical profile can result in unfair advantage during competition. This surveillance strategy is largely the unfortunate outcome of a sports culture dominated by masculine privileging, in which the unexamined association of maleness and physicality has led to the belief that "sporting prowess contradict[s] womanhood" (Pieper 2016b: 1). As Eileen McDonagh and Laura Pappano (2007: 40) observe, since "male performance is the standard against which female performance is measured," poorly performing men are often derogatorily called "girls," whereas women who perform exceedingly well see their femaleness questioned. "Suspicious" bodies that contradict the Western, (cis) sexist paradigm of "female athletes in huggable packages" (Kaplan quoted in Pieper 2016b: 106) are thus submitted to "visual judgments by onlookers from the Global North" (Henne 2015: 112–13).

Gender verification is founded on the assumption that, "with enough scrutiny, one's 'true gender' can be revealed at the level of the body" (Beauchamp 2009: 358). However, as previously noted, "human biology does not break down into male and female as politely as sport governing bodies wish it would" (Epstein 2014: 58). Verification methods have varied over time, in ways that reflected progressive discoveries in chromosomal science and resulting shifts in understandings of sex and gender, including the "continued medico-scientific interpretation of womanhood" (Pieper 2016b: 184). Initially, anatomical examinations known as "naked parades" prioritized the visual inspection of external genitalia (Erikainen 2019), which are believed to "play the role of 'concealed truth' about a person's sex" (Bettcher 2007: 48). However, as the case of Spanish hurdler Maria José Martinez-Patiño famously proved, some women could possess "female" sex organs *and* a Y chromosome—that is, pass a "naked parade" but fail a sex chromatin or DNA test (Erikainen 2019). Currently, gender verification emphasizes the "science of testosterone" (Jordan-Young and Karkazis 2019: 223). The latest parameters have been discussed extensively in relation to the increased visibility of trans sportswomen, who must demonstrate physiological equivalency with cisgender athletes (i.e., comparable testosterone levels) to compete (Gleaves and Lehrbach 2016). Even so, current eligibility regulations fail to consider that "hormonal profiles do not fit neatly into binary sex-segregated competition categories" (MacKinnon 2017: 43). Furthermore, no causal relationship has been identified between higher endogenous testosterone levels—allegedly the primary cause of gaps between male and female performances—and improved athletic function, making testosterone "a hopeless unreliable predictor of performance in post-puberty athletes" (Ivy and Conrad 2018: 133).

Sex testing has long been denounced as unnecessary, degrading, and misogynistic (Pieper 2016a). It is known to have caused feelings of shame and isolation, depression, and even suicide among the affected athletes (Wiesemann 2011). Furthermore, all verification methods have yielded inconclusive, contradictory, and even erroneous results (Pieper 2016b). Laura A. Wackwitz (2003) contends that the earliest instances of sex testing date back to the ancient Olympics, in which men would compete fully naked to prove their maleness in the most straightforward fashion. As Florence Ashley (2018: 369) points out, "The ideal trans subject is naked" as well, readily lending itself to the prurient gazing of ruthless spectators. Indeed, although predominantly discussed in regard to sports, gender verification has been a preeminent tool of transmisogynistic interpellation of the body. Whether taking place at the doctor's or in the dangerous privacy of intimate encounters, sex tests reinforce the construction of the "body as site of truth" (Willox quoted in Barker-Plummer 2013: 719), with critical and oftentimes murderous reverberations. As Talia Mae Bettcher (2007: 47) writes, "Transphobic violence may be understood in terms of the related notions of 'exposure,' 'discovery,' 'appearance,' and 'reality.'" Sadly, it is not uncommon for pre- or non-op transgender women to be killed by their intimate partners following the forced inspection of their birth organs. However, the "centrality of genitals as sex determining" (59) within dating scenarios is also progressively threatened by a more dispersed conceptualization of the sexed/gendered body that betrays the "impossibility of locating the exact boundaries of womanhood" (Pieper 2016b: 101). In fact, this conceptual shift mirrors the trajectory of sex testing development rather accurately. Like athletes who could pass a "naked parade" but not a chromosomal test, transgender women who have undergone gender confirmation surgery (GCS)—a procedure that "forces rejection of either genital essentiality or the invariance of sex" (Bettcher 2007: 49)—might "pass" a visual inspection as cisgender and date as such. Once the locus of investigation is transferred further inside the body to evaluate nonvisual parameters, the concept of "physiological equivalency" returns in the shape of passing privilege: "resemblance" to a cisgender female standard, in the very same form of comparable hormonal profiles, becomes decisive in delivering "proof" of womanhood. However, regardless of appearance, "one might cite chromosomes as a way of claiming that a transperson is 'really a so and so'" (49). I have heard many heterosexual men declare that they would not date a trans woman "even" if she had had GCS and passed as cisgender, simply because she "used to be a man." Many others would forbid trans women from competing in elite sports even if they met physiological equivalency requirements, citing the indelibility of "muscle memory" (Torres et al. 2022: 36). Ultimately, in sports as in dating, "which features ought to be used to determine sex (e.g., chromosomes, identity, genitalia) is a matter of some dispute . . . in cases in which they are at odds with each other" (Bettcher 2007: 63). In this sense, transgender embodiment rejects univocal understandings of not only gender but also sexual orientation. Are heterosexual men attracted to "female" genitalia or to womanhood and femininity? And if male heterosexuality can indeed be reduced to attraction to female genitals, why would surgically reconstructed ones not count? One could cite infertility as a reason for refusing to date trans women and thus ground orientation in reproductive apparatuses rather than genitalia. But would that make a man's attraction to a cisgender infertile woman nonheterosexual? Clearly, sexual orientation, especially when genitals based, does not always fully account for rejection. I would argue that, within dating contexts, fears of unerasable male traces lead many to reject trans women, owing to their allegedly retaining a sort of "gender memory." When a trans woman fails to make such gender memory strategically known to her intimate partner(s), that nondisclosure becomes a crime of deception.

Deception

Transgender embodiment has long been framed as inherently fraudulent. Joelle Ruby Ryan (2009: 65) posits that "the transgender body, which mixes signifiers in unique and sometimes startling ways, is hegemonically constructed as always already deceptive and duplicitous. To many societal actors, the transgender body 'lies' because of its perceived disunity between bodily surface, gender expression, and erotic interest." Similarly, Serano (2007: 247–48) has argued that deception is "the noose that the narcissistic drape around the necks of transgender women . . . the scarlet letter that trans people are made to wear so that everybody else can claim innocence." Trans sportswomen are routinely charged with faking womanhood to build prestige dishonestly (Sharrow 2021), and they are even compared to able-bodied athletes feigning disabilities to earn medals at the Paralympic Games (Cavanagh and Sykes 2006). It is no accident that Fallon Fox was not only criticized for competing in the women's division but also publicly shamed for not making her transness immediately visible. Ashlee Evans-Smith explained that Fox "did have an advantage . . . but I took the fight knowing that" and found it "insulting that she didn't let us know initially" (MMA Interviews 2013).

Central to exclusionary arguments is the allegation that trans women retain male patterns of violence (Wild 2019) and live as "predators in prey's attire"—a concern clearly "predicated upon the identification of penis with rapist" (Bettcher 2007: 57). These assumptions align with cultural readings of trans women as harassers in disguise (Serano 2007) and sport competitions as sites where dangerous hormonal violence is redirected into a socially acceptable form (Miller 2007). A mixed-race trans athlete like Fox endures triple scrutiny. First, as a trans woman, she must contend with the insinuation that trans women are actually men invading women's spaces with criminal intent. Second, as non-White, she faces a history of racist claims of difference in bone density (Fausto-Sterling 2008). Third, as a trans woman of color, she is the target of stigmatizing conceptions of a primitive, bestial Black masculinity that is naturally prone to physical and sexual violence (Davis 1981; Hoch 1979). In this sense, her "deception" does not concern gender alone, but the masking of her alleged dangerousness as well.

It is perhaps in this climate of sexual panics and related fears of deception that the overlap between anti-trans stigma in sports and in dating becomes most evident. In dating contexts, trans women are frequently accused of, again, feigning womanhood to trick straight men or lesbians into sex and romance. Exclusionary factions of the lesbian community increasingly support this view. Building on Janice Raymond's (1979: 104) infamous argument that "all transsexuals rape women's bodies," radical feminist groups have framed trans inclusion in lesbian communities as "a viciously toxic form of men's sexual rights activism that has managed to rebrand and reframe itself as a civil rights movement" (Yardley 2018). While lesbians' dating preferences in relation to trans women are yet to be addressed in scholarly research, members of the exclusionary fringes have reported feeling "paranoid that someone [they] could match with could be a man," "unsafe at the thought of going on a date with a man," and essentially "betrayed," "violated," and "fooled" (Wild 2019: 10). Trans women are being accused of pressuring young lesbians into sex (Lowbridge 2021). Black men encountered a similar fate in the past; for instance, when the sexual assault charges levelled against prominent Black male athletes gained exceptional media attention (Enck-Wanzer 2009).

Lastly, as Alex Sharpe (2016) and Ashley (2018) have documented, in some jurisdictions failure or unwillingness to notify sexual partners of one's trans status prior to engaging in sex can amount to rape by vitiated consent, or rape by deception. Such was the line of reasoning employed by the defense team of Araujo's killers. In fact, in a "legal and cultural world in which transgender and deception are viewed as synonymous" (Sharpe 2016: 40), it is unsurprising that the judicial system that we expect to protect us relies on the very same flawed premises of the violence it seeks to prevent. In murder trials, trans panic defense strategies foreground a trans person's passing ability as the "perpetration of an identity-based fraud" (Billard 2019: 468). Through the heinous exercise of "murder-excusing and blame-shifting rhetoric" (Bettcher 2007: 44), the victim's nondisclosure, rather than the perpetrator's violent reaction, is criminalized for "exposing others to accidental homosexuality" (Ashley 2018: 353). As Serano (2007: 248) sarcastically asks, "Why challenge our culture's myopic view of male sexuality when it's so easy to blame it all on one deceiving tranny?"

Anxiously Close: Concluding Remarks

Toby Miller (2007) has argued that sex and sports are "forever intertwined." Both entail physical performance. Both require awareness of and connection to one's own body as well as others'. Both can foster a sense of safety, well-being, and belonging, or generate distress, self-doubt, and frustration. Crucially, both entertain fraught relations with questions pertaining to gendered embodiment. In overlapping ways, sex and sports are sites of bodily intimacy where specific eligibility requirements are introduced, the centrality of consent and fair play is emphasized, and the cultural meanings of gender are perpetually negotiated. Letitia Anne Peplau, Zick Rubin, and Charles T. Hill (1977: 106) note that physical intimacy is initially established by following social scripts based on "shared rules learned from the culture" rather than instinctual or spontaneous interactions. Transgender embodiment is bound to violate the cisnormative grammar of such scripts and ask uncomfortable questions around intimacy. Through physicality, "people make statements about their individual and social identities, and they also make inferences about the sort of people their partners are" (106). To conceive of "fair," consensual intimate scenarios between cisgender and transgender bodies without evoking the menace of physical or sexual violation at the hands of the latter is made to appear a hopeless endeavor. As trans bodies take on suspicious, deceitful, and even nefarious connotations, the space of intimacy easily transforms into a crime scene. It is no coincidence that some transgender individuals have been formally charged with "obtaining sexual intimacy by fraud" (Sharpe 2014: 207). This bizarrely formulated offense speaks volumes about both the assumption that trans people hold no right to participate in intimacy with other (cis) bodies and the accusation that the only way they can access the world of sexual pleasures is through illicit, predatory behavior.

Of course, dating contexts are varied and complex. There are countless (cis) men and women out there who enjoy dating transgender women; enthusiastic, safe, "fair" cis-trans body intimacy can and does exist. Additionally, trans women may partner with other trans folks or individuals whose orientation is multisexual; while such situations are not addressed here, they are common. In fact, it is cisgender heterosexual men and homosexual women who express "overwhelmingly exclusionary" dating preferences (Blair and Hoskin 2019: 2083), which makes these two demographics especially relevant to the present discussion. When it comes to intimacy, there is a tendency to label the matter as a strictly private one. To be sure, sexual preferences are not invariantly tied to the naturalization of "taste" or to the conflation of sexual orientation (e.g., lesbian) and specific organs (e.g., vagina). Some women might legitimately refuse to date non- or preoperative transgender women, owing to past sexual trauma. Similarly, domestic abuse survivors might look askance at transfeminine inclusion in sports as it continues to be framed as state-sanctioned male violence. These are delicate questions that deserve careful consideration. The conversation needs to accommodate both a plurality of identities and everyone's right to free association. However, this is precisely why the debate matters. In such a vitriolic climate, reflecting on the nature of our "preferences" can benefit all of us. Anti-trans propaganda is actively feeding into the scaremongering that trans people think they are owed sex and therefore demand intimacy with cisgender folks in order to feel validated in their own identity. However, not only does this belief overlook the fact that transgender people are notoriously more likely to be victims than perpetrators of violent crimes, but it also conceals the reality that entire systems of oppression, masked as private matters, are operating with impunity.

It is notable that, at the same time as transgender participation in sports has become widely discussed, at least two dating "movements" have emerged whose manifestos are organized specifically around the categorical refusal of cistrans intimacy. In early 2021 thousands of TikTok, Reddit, and Twitter users instituted "Super Straight" sexuality, comprising men and women who are only attracted to cisgender persons of the opposite sex. A TikTok user who was "sick of being labelled with very negative terms for having a preference, something I can't control" coined the term, which rapidly snowballed into a full-fledged movement; shortly before being taken down, the "r/superstraight" subreddit was on its way to reaching thirty thousand members (Kumar 2021). Central to the super straight argument is the belief that heterosexuality is somehow being diluted and debauched by the presence of transgender women (and men) in heterosexual dating venues; hence the perceived insufficiencies of *straight* in capturing exclusionary "taste" and the need to prefix the word to reinforce its meaning. Some super straights even condemned trans people's alleged sense of entitlement to cis bodies as "rapey" and akin to that found among incel communities (Collins 2021).

The main tenets of the super straight philosophy are rather similar to those of the trans-exclusionary or gender critical factions of the lesbian community, which have also been vocal about not wanting trans women to "infiltrate" lesbian dating spheres. Although instances of trans exclusion from certain lesbian spaces are not a new phenomenon (Earles 2019), they have become more prominent in recent years. Here, allusions to the same allegedly "rapey" attitude of transfeminine daters have led to the specious argument that trans inclusion in the lesbian sphere is merely a manifestation of the patriarchal policing of lesbian sexuality, and an attempt at erasing lesbian identity. In particular, the perceived appropriation of lesbian identity by non- or pre-operative trans women has been juxtaposed to past modalities of lesbophobic repression, including conversion therapy and corrective rape. The argument goes back to the "rape by deception" lamented by the heterosexual cisgender men who appeal to the trans panic defense.

As Serano (2007: 239) notes, "Some of the most common arguments used to deny trans women the right to participate in women-only spaces also happen to be the most antifeminist." To equate the presence of a penis (or whatever "male traces" are presumed to linger in post-op trans women) to the threat of feminization/homosexualization (super straight) or to patriarchal oppression (exclusionary lesbian communities) is to assume, at best, a blatantly essentialist and phallocentric stance. Additionally, the fact that some of these movements are geographically widespread, heavily politicized, and even linked to far-right ideologies should give us a sense of what is truly at stake here. Elizabeth A. Sharrow (2021: 5) argues that "surveillance of transgender people is often most acute where sex-based identities are the most salient." The highly gendered, intensely policed domains of sports and dating instantiate how, when it comes to transgender exclusion, nearsighted notions of sex and biology are, with a few legitimate exceptions, a red herring. Instead, the regulation of biological citizenship in conformity to "the Western, Olympic, imperial white imaginations['s] . . . desire for corporeal homogeneity, bio-centric gender demarcation and stable corporeal body boundaries" (Cavanagh and Sykes 2006: 97) is a key factor. At the same time, gender-dictated "body boundaries" are inextricably entangled with racialized and nationalist ones, for "bodies may be read as gender deviant in relation to racial, religious, and/or national appearance" as well (Beauchamp 2019: 6). Germane to this concept is a quote by transgender writer Patrick Califia: "Prejudice usually can't survive close contact with the people who are supposed to be so despicable, which is why the propagandists for hate always preach separation" (quoted in Serano 2007: 233). Some sports and dating communities have already embraced their own radical "queering" and are thriving on transgender inclusion. Others still have a long way to go. To understand how to bring all bodies together, we must not lose sight of the shared mechanisms that are keeping them apart.

Tristan Venturi is an independent scholar whose main areas of research interest fall at the intersection of media studies and queer studies. After earning his BA in communications magna cum laude from John Cabot University in 2016, Tristan went on to pursue graduate studies at King's College London, where he obtained his MA (Dist.) in film studies in 2021. Tristan specializes in film and audiovisual studies, women's and gender studies, and queer and transgender theory. His current research interests include the exploration of cinematic and televisual representations of transgender embodiment as inherently deceptive, as well as the Italian media coverage of transgender citizenship in relation to anti-gender movements and populist notions of Italianness.

References

a_dolf_please. 2021. "How to filter trans people from matches?" Reddit, July 11. https://www.reddit .com/r/Tinder/comments/oi65p9/how_to_filter_trans_people_from_matches/.

Anderson, Eric, and Travers. 2017. *Transgender Athletes in Competitive Sport*. London: Routledge.

Anderson, Veanne. 2018. "Cisgender Men and Trans Prejudice: Relationships with Sexual Orientation and Gender Self-Esteem." *Psychology of Men and Masculinity* 19, no. 3: 373–84. http://doi.org/10.1037/men0000125.

Ashley, Florence. 2018. "Genderfucking Non-disclosure: Sexual Fraud, Transgender Bodies, and Messy Identities." *Dalhousie Law Journal* 41, no. 2: 340–77. https://digitalcommons .schulichlaw.dal.ca/dlj/vol41/iss2/3/.

Bahrampour, Tara, Scott Clement, and Emily Guskin. 2022. "Most Americans Oppose Trans Athletes in Female Sports, Poll Finds." *Washington Post*, June 14. https://www.washington post.com/dc-md-va/2022/06/13/washington-post-umd-poll-most-americans-oppose -transgender-athletes-female-sports/.

Bailey, Moya, and Trudy. 2018. "On Misogynoir: Citation, Erasure, and Plagiarism." *Feminist Media Studies* 18, no. 4: 762-768. https://doi.org/10.1080/14680777.2018.1447395.

Barker-Plummer, Bernadette. 2013. "Fixing Gwen. News and the Mediation of (Trans)gender Challenges." *Feminist Media Studies* 13, no. 4: 710–24. https://doi.org/10.1080/14680777 .2012.679289.

Beauchamp, Toby. 2009. "Artful Concealment and Strategic Visibility: Transgender Bodies and U.S. State Surveillance after 9/11." *Surveillance and Society* 6, no. 4: 356–66. https://ojs .library.queensu.ca/index.php/surveillance-and-society/article/view/3267.

Beauchamp, Toby. 2019. *Going Stealth: Transgender Politics and U.S. Surveillance Practices*. Durham, NC: Duke University Press.

Bettcher, Talia Mae. 2007. "Evil Deceivers and Make-Believers: On Transphobic Violence and the Politics of Illusion." *Hypatia* 22, no. 3: 43–65. https://www.jstor.org/stable/4640081.

Billard, Thomas. 2019. "'Passing' and the Politics of Deception: Transgender Bodies, Cisgender Aesthetics, and the Policing of Inconspicuous Marginal Identities." In *The Palgrave Handbook of Deceptive Communication*, edited by Tony Docan-Morgan, 463–77. https://doi.org /10.1007/978-3-319-96334-1_24.

Blair, Karen L., and Rhea Ashley Hoskin. 2019. "Transgender Exclusion from the World of Dating: Patterns of Acceptance and Rejection of Hypothetical Trans Dating Partners as a Function of Sexual and Gender Identity." *Journal of Social and Personal Relationships* 36, no. 7: 2074–95. https://doi.org/10.1177/0265407518779139.

Buggs, Shantel Gabrieal. 2020. "(Dis)Owning Exotic: Navigating Race, Intimacy, and Trans Identity." *Sociological Inquiry* 90, no. 2: 249–70. https://doi.org/10.1111/soin.12348.

Cavanagh, Sheila L., and Heather Sykes. 2006. "Transsexual Bodies at the Olympics: The International Olympic Committee's Policy on Transsexual Athletes at the 2004 Athens Summer Games." *Body and Society* 12, no. 3: 75–102. https://10.1177/1357034X06067157.

Cleland, Jamie, Ellis Cashmore, and Kevin Dixon. 2021. "Why Do Sports Fans Support or Oppose the Inclusion of Trans Women in Women's Sports? An Empirical Study of Fairness and Gender Identity." *Sports in Society* 25, no. 12: 2381–96. https://doi.org/10.1080/17430437.2021.1942456.

Collins, Sam. 2021. "Super Straight?" YouTube video, 16:19. Uploaded March 7. https://www.youtube.com/watch?v=6MkwXKn0RjQ.

Davis, Angela Y. 1981. *Women, Race, and Class.* New York: Random House.

Dowling, Colette. 2000. *The Frailty Myth: Women Approaching Physical Equality.* New York: Random House.

Earles, Jennifer. 2019. "The 'Penis Police': Lesbian and Feminist Spaces, Trans Women, and the Maintenance of the Sex/Gender/Sexuality System." *Journal of Lesbian Studies* 23, no. 2: 243–56. https://doi.org/10.1080/10894160.2018.1517574.

Enck-Wanzer, Suzanne Marie. 2009. "All's Fair in Love and Sport: Black Masculinity and Domestic Violence in the News." *Communication and Critical/Cultural Studies* 6, no. 1: 1–18. https://doi.org/10.1080/14791420802632087.

Epstein, David. 2014. *The Sports Gene: Inside the Science of Extraordinary Athletic Performance.* New York: Penguin Group.

Erikainen, Sonja. 2019. *Gender Verification and the Making of the Female Body in Sport: A History of the Present.* London: Routledge.

Esposito, Mario. 2022. "Lo picchia con forza 'sospetta' e lui scopre che è trans." *Occhio notizie*, March 8. https://www.occhionotizie.it/picchia-fidanzato-carrara-transessuale-ristorante/.

Fairchild, Phaylen. 2022. "Activists Attacking Trans Athletes Keep Targeting Cis Women Instead." *Medium*, March 21. https://aninjusticemag.com/activists-attacking-trans-athletes-keep-targeting-cis-women-instead-cb6948e6a9fe.

Fausto-Sterling, Anne. 2000. *Sexing the Body: Gender Politics and the Construction of Sexuality.* New York: Basic.

Fausto-Sterling, Anne. 2008. "The Bare Bones of Race." *Social Studies of Science* 38, no. 5: 657–94. https://www.jstor.org/stable/25474604.

Fischer, Mia, and Jennifer McClearen. 2020. "Transgender Athletes and the Queer Art of Athletic Failure." *Communication and Sport* 8, no. 2: 147–67. https://doi.org/10.1177/2167479518823207.

Flores, Andrew, Donald Haider-Markel, Daniel Lewis, Patrick Miller, Barry Tadlock, and Jami Taylor. 2020. "Public Attitudes about Transgender Participation in Sports: The Roles of Gender, Gender Identity Conformity, and Sports Fandom." *Sex Roles* 83, nos. 5–6: 382–98. https://doi.org/10.1007/s11199-019-01114-z.

Gamarel, Kristi, Laura Jadwin-Cakmak, Wesley King, Ashley Lacombe-Duncan, Racquelle Trammell, Lilianna Reyes, Cierra Burks, Bré Rivera, Emily Arnold, and Gary Harper. 2022. "Stigma Experienced by Transgender Women of Color in Their Dating and Romantic Relationships: Implications for Gender-Based Violence Prevention Programs." *Journal of Interpersonal Violence* 37, nos. 9–10: 8161–89. https://pubmed.ncbi.nlm.nih.gov/33256510/.

Gleaves, John, and Tim Lehrbach. 2016. "Beyond Fairness: The Ethics of Inclusion for Transgender and Intersex Athletes." *Journal of the Philosophy of Sport* 43, no. 2: 311–26. https://doi.org/10.1080/00948705.2016.1157485.

Global Sport Institute at Arizona University, and OH Predictive Insights. 2021. "National Sports Public Opinion Pulse Update." May. globalsport.asu.edu/sites/default/files/resources/gsi _national_snapshot_poll_summer_2021_key_takeaways.pdf.

Griffin, Pat. 1998. *Strong Women, Deep Closets: Lesbians and Homophobia in Sport*. Champaign, IL: Human Kinetics.

Hanley, Christine, and Jessica Garrison. 2002. "More Told in Teen's Killing." *Los Angeles Times*, October 22. https://www.latimes.com/archives/la-xpm-2002-oct-22-me-eddie22-story .html.

Henne, Kathryn E. 2015. *Testing for Athlete Citizenship: Regulating Doping and Sex in Sport*. New Brunswick, NJ: Rutgers University Press.

Hoch, Paul. 1979. *White Hero, Black Beast*. London: Pluto.

Human Rights Foundation. 2021. *Dismantling a Culture of Violence*. Updated October 2021. https://reports.hrc.org/dismantling-a-culture-of-violence.

Iantaffi, Alex, and Walter O. Bockting. 2011. "Views from Both Sides of the Bridge? Gender, Sexual Legitimacy, and Transgender People's Experiences of Relationships." *Culture, Health, and Sexuality* 13, no. 3: 355–70. https://doi.org/10.1080/13691058.2010.537770.

Iole, Kevin. 2013. "UFC Suspends Matt Mitrione for Transphobic Comments Regarding Fallon Fox." *Yahoo Sports*, April 9. https://sports.yahoo.com/blogs/mma-cagewriter/ufc-suspends -matt-mitrione-transphobic-comments-regarding-fallon-230051067--mma.html.

Ivy, Veronica, and Aryn Conrad. 2018. "Including Trans Women Athletes in Competitive Sport: Analyzing the Science, Law, and Principles and Policies of Fairness in Competition." *Philosophical Topics* 46, no. 2: 103–40. https://www.jstor.org/stable/10.2307/26927952.

Jones, Bethany Alice, Jon Arcelus, Walter Pierre Bouman, and Emma Haycraft. 2017. "Sport and Transgender People: A Systematic Review of the Literature Relating to Sport Participa- tion and Competitive Sport Policies." *Sports Med* 47, no. 4: 701–16. https://doi.org/10.1007 /s40279-016-0621-y.

Jordan-Young, Rebecca, and Katrina Karkazis. 2019. *Testosterone: An Unauthorized Biography*. Cambridge, MA: Harvard University Press.

JRE Clips. 2018a. "Joe Rogan Reflects on Fallon Fox Controversy." YouTube video, 18:56. Uploaded July 26. https://www.youtube.com/watch?v=KQpQmNhya14.

JRE Clips 2018b. "You're a Bigot If You Don't Want to Date a Trans Woman? Joe Rogan and Jordan Peterson." YouTube video, 6:35. Uploaded December 8. https://www.youtube .com/watch?v=sCpqcHb-5yA.

Karkazis, Katrina. 2016. "The Ignorance Aimed at Caster Semenya Flies in the Face of the Olympic Spirit." *Guardian*, August 23. https://www.theguardian.com/commentisfree/2016/aug/23 /caster-semenya-olympic-spirit-iaaf-athletes-women.

Karkazis, Katrina, and Rebecca M. Jordan-Young. 2018. "The Powers of Testosterone: Obscuring Race and Regional Bias in the Regulation of Women Athletes." *Feminist Formations* 30, no. 2: 1–39. https://doi.org/10.1353/ff.2018.0017.

Kumar, Jaishree. 2021. "Inside the 'Super Straight' Movement That Got Banned on TikTok and Reddit." *Vice*, March 24. https://www.vice.com/en/article/5dp793/superstraight-sexuality -movement-transphobia-reddit-tiktok.

Lowbridge, Caroline. 2021. "The Lesbians Who Feel Pressured to Have Sex and Relationships with Trans Women." BBC, October 26. https://www.bbc.co.uk/news/uk-england-57853385.

Lucas, Cathryn B., and Kristine E. Newhall. 2018. "Out of the Frame: How Sports Media Shapes Trans Narratives." In *LGBT Athletes in the Sports Media*, edited by Rory Magrath, 99–124. London: Palgrave Macmillan.

MacKinnon, Kinnon. 2017. "An Introduction to Five Exceptional Trans Athletes from around the World." In *Transgender Athletes in Competitive Sport*, edited by Eric Anderson and Travers, 43–53. London: Routledge.

Mao, Jessica, Mara Haupert, and Eliot Smith. 2018. "How Gender Identity and Transgender Status Affect Perceptions of Attractiveness." *Social Psychological and Personality Science* 10, no. 6: 811–22. https://doi.org/10.1177/1948550618783716.

McCarthy, Justin. 2021. "Mixed Views among Americans on Transgender Issues." Gallup, May 26. https://news.gallup.com/poll/350174/mixed-views-among-americans-transgender-issues .aspx.

McDonagh, Eileen, and Laura Pappano. 2007. *Playing with the Boys: Why Separate Is Not Equal in Sports*. New York: Oxford University Press.

Messner, Michael A. 1988. "Sports and Male Domination: The Female Athlete as Contested Ideological Terrain." *Sociology of Sport Journal* 5, no. 3: 197–211. https://doi.org/10.1123/ssj .5.3.197.

Miller, Toby. 2007. "Sports and Sex, Forever Intertwined." *Outsports*, March 5. https://www .outsports.com/2013/4/6/4192358/sports-and-sex-forever-intertwined.

MMA Interviews. 2013. "Ashlee Evans-Smith Says She Feels Fallon Fox Shouldn't Be Able to Fight Women." YouTube video, 9:11. Posted November 2018. https://www.youtube.com/watch ?v=TRBGnjoWdo8.

Mocarski, Richard, Robyn King, Sim Butler, Natalie R. Holt, T. Zachary Huit, Debra A. Hope, Heather M. Meyer, and Nathan Woodruff. 2019. "The Rise of Transgender and Gender Diverse Representation in the Media: Impacts on the Population." *Communication, Culture, and Critique* 12, no. 3: 416–33. 10.1093/ccc/tcz031.

Parker, Richard G., and John H. Gagnon. 1995. *Conceiving Sexuality: Approaches to Sex Research in a Postmodern World*. New York: Routledge.

Pastor, Aaren. 2019. "Unwarranted and Invasive Scrutiny: Caster Semenya, Sex-Gender Testing, and Production of Woman in 'Women's' Track and Field." *Feminist Review* 122, no. 1: 1–15. https://doi.org/10.1177%2F0141778919849688.

Pearce, Ruth, Sonja Erikainen, and Ben Vincent. 2020. "TERF Wars: An Introduction." *Sociological Review* 68, no. 4: 677–98. https://doi.org/10.1177/0038026120934713.

Peplau, Letitia Anne, Zick Rubin, and Charles T. Hill. 1977. "Sexual Intimacy in Dating Relationships." *Journal of Social Issues* 33, no. 2: 86–109. https://doi.org/10.1111/j.1540-4560 .1977.tb02007.x.

PhriekModeUSA. 2021. Comment on mosesyastrzemski, "Question: Is there a way to omit trans people from my Tinder feed?" Reddit, October 12. https://www.reddit.com/r/Tinder /comments/q6tlfh/question_is_there_a_way_to_omit_trans_people_from/.

Pieper, Lindsay Parks. 2016a. "'Preserving la Difference': The Elusiveness of Sex-Segregated Sport." *Sport in Society* 19, nos. 8–9: 1138–55. https://doi.org/10.1080/17430437.2015.1096258.

Pieper, Lindsay Parks. 2016b. *Sex Testing: Gender Policing in Women's Sports*. Urbana: University of Illinois Press.

Pilgrim, Jill, David Martin, and Will Binder. 2003. "Far from the Finish Line: Transsexualism and Athletic Competition." *Fordham Intellectual Property, Media and Entertainment Law Journal* 13, no. 2: 496–549. https://ir.lawnet.fordham.edu/iplj/vol13/iss2/4.

Raymond, Janice. 1979. *The Transsexual Empire: The Making of the She-Male*. Boston: Beacon.

Reed, Erin (@erininthemorn). 2022. "We can always tell." Twitter, March 20. https://twitter.com /ErinInTheMorn/status/1505636800437669897.

Riaz, Adnan. 2021. "'What the F**k Has MMA Become?'—Alana McLaughlin Hits Back at Troll's Vile Now-Deleted Transphobic Tweet." *Sports Bible*, September 20. https://www.sportbible.com/mma/alana-mclaughlin-hits-back-at-twitter-trolls-vile-transphobic-tweet-20210920.

Rubin, Gayle S. 2006. "Thinking Sex: Notes for a Radical Theory of the Politics of Sexuality." In *Culture, Society, and Sexuality: A Reader*, edited by Richard Parker and Peter Aggleton, 150–87. London: Routledge. https://doi.org/10.4324/9780203966105.

Ryan, Joelle Ruby. 2009. "Reel Gender: Examining the Politics of Trans Images in Film and Media." PhD diss., Bowling Green State University. https://www.proquest.com/docview/30484 5566/fulltextPDF/6E50447E018A45B5PQ/1.

Schilt, Kristen, and Laurel Westbrook. 2015. "Bathroom Battlegrounds and Penis Panics." *Contexts* 14, no. 3: 26–31. https://doi.org/10.1177/1536504215596943.

Serano, Julia. 2007. *Whipping Girl: A Transsexual Woman on Sexism and the Scapegoating of Feminism*. Berkeley, CA: Seal.

Serano, Julia. 2012. "Trans-misogyny Primer." Julia Serano (blog), April 3. http://juliaserano.blogspot.com/2012/04/trans-misogyny-primer.html.

Sharpe, Alex. 2014. "Criminalising Sexual Intimacy: Transgender Defendants and the Legal Construction of Non-consent." *Criminal Law Review*, no. 3: 207–23. https://uk.westlaw.com/Document/IC3F60A41938211E38BD0C1ECC4AB239B/View/FullText.html.

Sharpe, Alex. 2016. "Expanding Liability for Sexual Fraud through the Concept of 'Active Deception': A Flawed Approach." *Journal of Criminal Law* 80, no. 1: 28–44. https://doi.org/10.1177/0022018315623674.

Sharrow, Elizabeth A. 2021. "Sports, Transgender Rights, and the Bodily Politics of Cisgender Supremacy." *Laws* 10, no. 63. https://doi.org/10.3390/laws10030063.

Snorton, Riley C. 2017. *Black on Both Sides: A Racial History of Trans Identity*. Minneapolis: University of Minnesota Press.

Torres, Cesar, Francisco Javier Loper Frias, and María José Martínez Patiño. 2022. "Beyond Physiology: Embodied Experience, Embodied Advantage, and the Inclusion of Transgender Athletes in Competitive Sport." *Sport, Ethics and Philosophy* 16, no. 1: 33–49. https://doi.org/10.1080/17511321.2020.1856915.

Travers. 2018. "Transgender Issues in Sports and Leisure." In *The Palgrave Handbook of Feminism and Sport, Leisure, and Physical Education*, edited by Louise Mansfield, Jayne Caudwell, Belinda Wheaton, and Beccy Watson, 649–65. London: Palgrave Macmillan.

Wackwitz, Laura A. 2003. "Verifying the Myth: Olympic Sex Testing and the Category 'Woman.'" *Women's Studies International Forum* 26, no. 6: 553–60. https://doi.org/10.1016/j.wsif.2003.09.009.

Westbrook, Laurel, and Kristen Schilt. 2013. "Doing Gender, Determining Gender: Transgender People, Gender Panics, and the Maintenance of the Sex/Gender/Sexuality System." *Gender and Society* 28, no. 1: 32–57. https://doi.org/10.1177%2F0891243213503203.

Wiesemann, Claudia. 2011. "Is There a Right Not to Know One's Sex? The Ethics of 'Gender Verification' in Women's Sports Competition." *Journal of Medical Ethics* 37, no. 4: 216–20. https://jme.bmj.com/content/37/4/216.

WikiHow. 2022. "Trying to Figure Out if Your Date Is Trans? Here's What You Should Consider." Last updated February 2023. https://www.wikihow.com/Know-if-Your-Date-is-Transgender.

Wild, Angela. 2019. "Lesbians at Ground Zero. Findings." *Get the L Out UK*, March 3. https://www.gettheloutuk.com/blog/category/research/lesbians-at-ground-zero.html.

Yardley, Miranda. 2018. "Girl Dick, the Cotton Ceiling, and the Cultural War on Lesbians and Women." *Medium*, December 9. https://medium.com/@mirandayardley/girl-dick-the -cotton-ceiling-and-the-cultural-war-on-lesbians-and-women-c323b4789368.

Zeigler, Cyd. 2013. "Fallon Fox Comes Out as Trans Pro MMA Fighter." *Outsports*, March 5. https:// www.outsports.com/2013/3/5/4068840/fallon-fox-trans-pro-mma-fighter.

Queer African Feminist Orientations for a Trans Sports Studies

ANIMA ADJEPONG

Abstract This commentary makes a case for developing trans sports studies out of queer African feminism. Queer African feminism is an epistemological orientation that affirms a flexible gender system, despite contemporary colonial gender ideologies, which insist on biological dimorphism. Queer African feminism offers to sports studies an analytical framework that attends to how colonialism, patriarchy, religion, and capitalism structure gender and sexual ideologies within sport and offers meaningful opportunities for disrupting these unjust systems. By centering the experiences of African athletes deemed intersex by sporting and medical authorities, the author demonstrates how current approaches to undermining sex segregation in sports still risk excluding certain athletes—intersex, nonbinary, and non-medically transitioning athletes. Ultimately, the author argues that if the goal of trans sports studies is to help bring about gender justice in sports, queer African feminism can offer a generative framework for attaining this goal.
Keywords queer African studies, coloniality of gender, intersex athletes, trans athletes, gender abolition

I n early May 2021, Ghanaian journalist Nuong Faalong aired an interview with aspiring national footballer, Holarli Ativor. The interview was an opportunity for Ativor to share her experiences of being dismissed from the Black Queens, the Ghanaian senior women's national team. Ativor explained that, although she qualified for the national team, once she arrived at camp, a medical exam declared her intersex. As she put it, "I was a footballer, but they said I was intersex so I can't compete with the women's side." Now, unemployed, she just "dey home." This medical intervention effectively ended Ativor's football career in 2019. Interspersed throughout the interview were conversations with Ativor's coach from the football academy and with a gynecologist presented as a gender expert. Speaking in Akan, Ativor's coach described her as a "lady." Affectionately referring to her as his child, the coach added that she is "overly aggressive," and although she played among women, a perceptive person might question if she was indeed a woman. Following this commentary from the coach, the doctor

TSQ: Transgender Studies Quarterly ★ Volume 10, Number 2 ★ May 2023
DOI 10.1215/23289252-10440790   © 2023 Duke University Press

explained that Ativor had what can be described as a disorder of sexual differentiation. Thus Ativor's intersex condition was used to explore gender expansiveness and also question the enforcement of surgery on people whose gender did not conform to the existing binary. In Faalong's words, "Is sports enough reason to put a well-functioning human through supposed corrective surgery?" Beyond surgery, this question can be extended to ask if athletes ought to endure hormonal treatments by suppressing their testosterone levels in order to play.

Annet Negesa, Castor Semenya, Bilguisa and Salimata Simpore, Holarli Ativor. These are just a few African athletes deemed not woman enough to compete in women's sports, despite having been raised as women and identifying as such. While intersex people are not de facto transgender, their experiences open up space to expansively think about the ideologies that sustain gendered surveillance within sport, maintain the gender binary, and exclude otherwise "well-functioning humans"[1] from sport participation. It bears noting that the overwhelming majority of intersex athletes we hear about are those assigned female at birth and subsequently excluded from women's sports (Pape 2020; Ritchie, Reynard, and Lewis 2008). This exclusion is not unlike transwomen's sport exclusion. The policing is meant to maintain strict and narrow definitions of who constitutes a woman, while also reifying the presumed superiority of masculinity. In this commentary, I consider the experiences of intersex athletes as a necessary component of thinking trans inclusion, which is to say gender-expansive inclusion, in sports. Intersex athletes are often subjected to unnecessary and unwanted medical interventions in order to take part in their respective sports. These medical interventions have lifelong consequences on their health and well-being (Negesa 2020). Critical engagement with the discourse surrounding intersex athletes' bodies demands a reorientation to gender in sports, and gender writ large. I enter this conversation as a sports scholar epistemologically grounded in queer African feminism. Consequently, some of my interventions might rehearse what trans studies scholars already know. However, if you stay with me to the end, you will find in this commentary an articulation of how a trans sports studies that critically engages queer African feminism moves us toward gender abolition.

Queer African Feminism, Gender beyond Binaries, and Sports Studies

Queer African feminism offers a different way of being and thinking that actively orients away from liberal feminist ideas of inclusion/equality and toward gender abolition. Within this epistemological perspective is an understanding that sex and gender as we experience them today are structured by persistent colonial logics, or coloniality. Coloniality describes the psychological and cultural legacies of colonization even after formal colonial structures have been overturned. The coloniality of gender, as Argentine feminist philosopher Maria Lugones (2008) termed it, maintains heterosexual patriarchy and biological dimorphism as universal truths about bodies and social organizations. Yet, as the foundational works of Ifi Amadiume (1987) and Oyèrónkẹ́ Oyěwùmí (1997) have taught us, in African societies, a flexible gender system refused the rigidity of binary sex and made possible a world in which those presumed to be women could take up space among men and vice versa (see also Murray and Roscoe 1998; Achebe 2011). The historically flexible gender system that characterized many African societies has not completely been eliminated, and instead exists in tandem with colonial gender ideologies. This fact is evident, for example, in how some working-class lesbians understand their gender (as women who are men) (for more on this see Dankwa 2021, in particular, chapter 3).

My engagement with queer African feminism considers the coloniality of gender while paying particular attention to those whose deviation from binary gender and heteronormativity severely disadvantages them within an already unequal economic system and social hierarchy. Here, the ways that the erotic offers opportunities to resist coloniality, patriarchy, and capitalism take center stage in my analysis (Adjepong 2022). Understanding the erotic as a manifestation of the political, sensual, and spiritual breaks apart rigid binaries that forestall the politics and pleasure inherent within sports. Elsewhere, I have written, "Taking a queer African studies approach to examining women's sports means paying attention to the homoerotic and the homophobic, the confluence of colonialism, patriarchy, Christianity, capitalist exploitation and opportunity; considering the unique consequences these structures have on women's sports and their generic effects on the sporting and cultural landscape more broadly" (Adjepong 2021: 281). This orientation to sports studies opens up meaningful space to redress the persistence of binary gender within sports and develop opportunities for culturally sensitive, justice-oriented approaches to sport inclusivity. Furthermore, such an approach moves us a step past the necessary reparations required to make sports equitable, and toward creating a space where desire and pleasure can be articulated and embodied beyond the confines of binary gender.

Feminist Sports Studies and the Reification of Binary Gender

Feminist sports studies have highlighted that, despite advances in women's access to sports, sports still often shore up heterosexual masculinity (Heywood and Dworkin 2003; Adjepong 2017; Ezzell 2009; Engh and Potgieter 2018). At the same time, women's participation in sports has challenged dominant ideas about women's bodies and femininity as docile and has created space for sportswomen to embody the full range of their physicality (Packer 2020; Beaver 2016; Broad 2001). The increasing visibility of trans sportswomen has presented heightened urgency around gender and sports inclusion, as evidenced by the number of recent publications and policy interventions made around this issue (Anderson and Travers 2017; Burke 2022; Harper 2022). The heightened urgency extends long-standing policing that has barred certain women from being readily and freely welcomed into women's sports because of their perceived gender and sexuality (Buzuvis 2013; Ritchie, Reynard, and Lewis 2008). The ongoing case of the South African runner, Caster Semenya, illustrates this point. Greater public attention directed toward transwomen's inclusion in sports, while necessary to address, illustrates how some of the current efforts toward developing gender justice in sports can reify the gender binary. In other words, the underlying issues of gender inequality caused by gender segregated sports are not addressed by the inclusion of transgender people into the current sporting landscape (Adjepong and Travers 2022).

A challenge for feminist sports scholars relying on Western epistemologies to do their work is that their approach to sports studies reifies binary gender. In part, this outcome is because liberal feminism has had the greatest impact on sports policies for women (Scraton and Flintoff 2002; Hall 1988). Liberal feminism is founded on the idea that women deserve the same rights as those that men supposedly naturally possess. As such, the focus of this political struggle is to ensure that women have opportunities equal to men's, sometimes ignoring the power structures that underpin gendered subordination. Furthermore, liberal feminism discounts differences in race, class, and gender expression to attain its goal of equality. Thus critical interventions that can create expansive gender inclusivity in sports are overlooked in favor of attaining equality with men. This intellectual-political orientation reifies binary gender and stultifies radical transformation to sports access.

Travers (2008) has proposed the abolition of men-only sporting spaces as a strategy for refusing the way that sports reproduces the gender binary, thus promoting gender justice. Writing about the role of "the sport nexus," or elite, male-dominated, sex segregated professional and amateur sport, Travers notes how this system normalizes and perpetuates a binary gender system with devastating consequences for women, girls, and LGBTQ athletes. This negative outcome for all but heterosexual cisgender men in sports is a direct result of how Western sports remains defined by, and a site for the production of, hegemonic masculinity. The abolition of men-only sporting spaces in favor of all-gender sites and voluntary segregation for women and girls begins to articulate a queer feminist strategy for gender justice in sports. Importantly, this approach does not neglect the implications of a long-standing exclusion of women from sports. However, it raises the question of whether transwomen would be welcome in these women-only spaces without (as happens now) requiring them to undergo surgeries or hormonal treatments. And what about the athletes introduced at the beginning of this commentary? Where would they be welcomed? A queer African feminist approach to redressing gender injustice in sports can attend to these questions. This analytical and political orientation to gender justice within sports takes redress into account while actively exploding the categories that created the need for such redress in the first place.

Conclusion

Creating more equitable sporting experiences must be grounded in feminist and anti-colonial principles. A trans sports studies that develops out of queer African feminism is well positioned to accomplish sporting inclusivity by shattering the gender binary. In this short intervention, I have not commented much on trans studies as an interdisciplinary formation and how those insights can (re)shape sports studies. I leave that intervention to trans studies scholars. Instead, as a queer African feminist scholar, I have invoked how indigenous epistemologies that challenge the coloniality of gender can help produce gender justice within sports. The experiences of athletes like Semenya, Ativor, Negesa, and the Simpores persist because of the gender binary, which marks their claim to womanness as suspect. That same binary also demands that trans athletes go through medical changes in order to take part in sports, whether at the professional or amateur level (e.g., schools). Yet an understanding of gender as a flexible system that does not inhere within bodies or produce hierarchies of physical ability presents a radical alternative to engaging sports. A trans sports studies that builds out of and on queer African feminism offers such an alternative. Within this framework, discourses of biological dimorphism that require medical interventions for athletes to participate in sports can be cast aside in favor of flexibility, respect, and inclusiveness, which affirms bodily autonomy, redresses historical systems of exclusion, and centers justice.

Anima Adjepong is assistant professor of women's, gender, and sexualities studies at the University of Cincinnati. They research, write, and teach about identity, culture, and social change and are particularly interested in how cultural struggles can bring about social transformation. Adjepong is the author of *Afropolitan Projects: Redefining Blackness, Sexualities, and Culture from Houston to Accra* (2021). They are currently working on a project about women's football, gendered nationalism, and state-sponsored homophobia in Ghana.

Acknowledgments

The author would like to thank Chandra Frank and Shannon Malone Gonzalez for their suggestions to improve this manuscript.

Note

1. The idea of a "well-functioning human" can be ableist if it normalizes what makes a person "well-functioning." Yet in this context, given that the journalist is speaking about Ativor as a woman despite medicalized claims that she is not, one can also read "well-functioning human" to mean that just as she is, there is nothing wrong with the athlete. As such, a generous engagement with this phrase can point toward a refusal of normalizing discourses that position certain bodies defective because they do not conform to ideals of gender, ability, etc.

References

Achebe, Nwando. 2011. *The Female King of Colonial Nigeria: Ahebi Ugbabe*. Bloomington: Indiana University Press.

Adjepong, Anima. 2017. "'We're, Like, a Cute Rugby Team': How Whiteness and Heterosexuality Shape Women's Sense of Belonging in Rugby." *International Review for the Sociology of Sport* 52, no. 2: 209–22. https://doi.org/10.1177/1012690215584092.

Adjepong, Anima. 2021. "For a Sociology of Women's Sports on the African Continent." In *Research Handbook on Sports and Society*, edited by Elizabeth C. K. Pike, 276–90. https://doi.org/10.4337/9781789903607.00030.

Adjepong, Anima. 2022. "Erotic Ethnography: Sex, Spirituality, and Embodiment in Qualitative Research." *Journal of Men's Studies* 30, no. 3: 383–401. https://doi.org/10.1177/10608265 221108201.

Adjepong, Anima, and Travers. 2022. "The Problem with Sex-Segregated Sports." *Society Pages*, December 9. https://thesocietypages.org/engagingsports/2022/12/09/the-problem-with -sex-segregated-sport/.

Amadiume, Ifi. 1987. *Male Daughters, Female Husbands: Gender and Sex in an African Society*. London: Zed.

Anderson, Eric, and Travers. 2017. *Transgender Athletes in Competitive Sport*. London: Routledge. *Transgender Athletes in Competitive Sport*. https://doi.org/10.4324/9781315304274.

Beaver, Travis. 2016. "Roller Derby Uniforms: The Pleasures and Dilemmas of Sexualized Attire." *International Review for the Sociology of Sport* 51, no. 6: 639–57.

Broad, KL. 2001. "The Gendered Unapologetic: Queer Resistance in Women's Sport." *Sociology of Sport Journal* 18, no. 2: 181–204.

Burke, Michael. 2022. "Trans Women Participation in Sport: A Commentary on the Conservatism of Gender Critical Feminism." *International Journal of Sport Policy and Politics* 14, no. 4: 689–96. https://doi.org/10.1080/19406940.2022.2101503.

Buzuvis, Erin E. 2013. "Transsexual and Intersex Athletes." In *Sexual Minorities in Sports: Prejudice at Play*, edited by Melanie L. Sartore-Baldwin, 55–72. Boulder, CO: Lynne Reinner. https://doi.org/10.1515/9781626370944-004.

Dankwa, Serena Owusua. 2021. *Knowing Women: Same-Sex Intimacy, Gender, and Identity in Postcolonial Ghana*. Cambridge: Cambridge University Press.

Engh, Mari Haugaa, and Cheryl Potgieter. 2018. "Hetero-Sexing the Athlete: Public and Popular Discourses on Sexuality and Women's Sport in South Africa." *Acta Academica* 50, no. 2: 34–51. https://doi.org/10.18820/24150479/AA50I2.2.

Ezzell, Matthew B. 2009. "'Barbie Dolls' on the Pitch: Identity Work, Defensive Othering, and Inequality in Women's Rugby." *Social Problems* 56, no. 1: 111–31.

Hall, Ann M. 1988. "The Discourse of Gender and Sport: From Femininity to Feminism." *Sociology of Sport Journal* 5: 330–40.

Harper, Joanna. 2022. "Transgender Athletes and International Sports Policy." *Law and Contemporary Problems* 85, no. 1: 151–65.

Heywood, Leslie, and Shari L. Dworkin. 2003. *Built to Win: The Female Athlete as Cultural Icon*. Minneapolis: University of Minnesota Press.

Lugones, Maria. 2008. "Coloniality of Gender." *Worlds and Knowledges Otherwise* 2, no. 2: 1–17.

Murray, Stephen O., and Will Roscoe. 1998. *Boy-Wives and Female Husbands: Studies in African Homosexualities*. Edited by Stephen O. Murray and Will Roscoe. New York: Palgrave.

Negesa, Annet. 2020. "The Story in Her Own Words." *Human Rights Defender* 29, no. 2: 36–37.

Oyěwùmí, Oyèrónké. 1997. *The Invention of Women: Making an African Sense of Western Gender Discourses*. Minneapolis: University of Minnesota Press.

Packer, Beth. 2020. "Moral Agency and the Paradox of Positionality: Disruptive Bodies and Queer Resistance in Senegalese Women's Soccer." In *Routledge Handbook of Queer African Studies*, edited by S. N. Nyeck, 129–41. London: Routledge.

Pape, Madeleine O. 2020. "The Unlevel Global Playing Field of Gender Eligibility Regulation in Sport." *Human Rights Defender* 29, no. 2: 41–43. https://search.informit.org/doi/epdf/10.3316/informit.386764603032909.

Ritchie, Robert, John Reynard, and Tom Lewis. 2008. "Intersex and the Olympic Games." *Journal of the Royal Society of Medicine* 101, no. 8: 395–99. https://doi.org/10.1258/jrsm.2008.080086.

Scraton, Sheila, and Anne Flintoff. 2002. "Sport Feminism: The Contribution of Feminist Thought to Our Understanding of Gender and Sport." In *Gender and Sport: A Reader*, edited by Sheila Scraton and Anne Flintoff, 30–46. London: Routledge.

Travers. 2008. "The Sport Nexus and Gender Injustice." *Studies in Social Justice* 2, no. 1: 79–101. https://doi.org/10.26522/ssj.v2i1.969.

STATEMENT

Good Hair, Bad Math

Breaking Apart Gender on a Figure Skating Pairs Team

ERICA RAND

Abstract While most policing of gender categorization in sport concerns a human unit of one, I've been maneuvering, since 2019, within a human unit of two, as part of a white, queer, gender-nonconforming pairs team with my figure skating partner Anna Kellar. Situating our training and activism within the growing movement for change in the sport, this piece considers some of our experiences, the challenges, and deep pleasures as we work to advance the skills and rule changes required to test and compete; to navigate racialized gender binarism and cis-heteronormitivity sedimented in training, rule, and custom; and to develop performance vocabularies to legibly represent queer gender.

Keywords figure skating, sport, queer gender, nonbinary

Most policing of gender categorization in sport concerns a human unit of one, judged as suitable or not to compete within a gender-segregated category. Since 2019 I've been maneuvering within a human unit of two, as part of a gender-nonconforming pairs team with my figure skating partner Anna Kellar. We are two white queer adult skaters. Anna is trans nonbinary. I function in skating officialdom as a cis woman, which I would simply have called my identity before being persuaded to rethink my allegiance to the category—but not my privilege within it—due to some physical changes of aging that reshaped my body and to persuasive critiques of "cis" as the exaltation of stasis, bodily gender assignment, and white supremacist, settler colonial binaries (Enke 2012: 69–70; Bey 2022: 21–24). Anna and I are one trick away—the pairs lift, which is coming!—from having the skills we need to compete at the lowest adult level in the system governed by US Figure Skating (USFS). Yet despite a notably ungendered definition of a pair in the USFS rule book, and the organization's publicized enthusiasm for queer and trans skaters, key gender requirements for testing and competition largely preclude our participation.

This piece shares some of our experiences as we work toward the skills and rule changes required to test and compete. While pairs figure skating is a meagerly populated discipline in a sport struggling to regain popularity, our experience is instructive more broadly about the knotted factors that entrench heteronormativity in regulation, representation, and training.

The section of the USFS Rulebook devoted to the "technical requirements" of pairs skating might perform the shortest flicker and dashing of hope anywhere in sport. The "Pair Definition," rule 7020 (out of 9,923; it's a rules-heavy sport), states, "Pair skating is the skating of two persons in unison who perform their movements in such harmony with each other as to give the impression of genuine pair skating as contrasted with independent single skating" (USFS 2022b: 213). So far so good, as far as gender inclusion goes, although some wiggle words like *harmony*, *impression*, or *genuine* might generate concern. The next sentence, striking in a rule book for its combination of vagueness and pride of place, is more alarming: "Attention should be paid to the selection of an appropriate partner." Paid by whom, and with what criteria? In a sport that retired only in 2021 the use of *ladies* as the official name for people competing as female, *appropriate* calls up respectability politics and the intertwined bigotries that have continued to plague figure skating, partly because of room for subjective judgment about appropriateness. For example, in all figure skating disciplines, "the clothing of the competitors must be modest, dignified and appropriate for athletic competitions and tests, not garish or theatrical in design" (rule 7031). Yet most people competing as female, including young children, wear skating dresses with super-short skirts and skin-colored "illusion fabric" that helps fake all sorts of skin reveal. How is that "modest and dignified" and not "garish or theatrical"? Meanwhile, "men must wear full-length trousers" (rule 7033). While a clarifying prohibition on tights was removed a few years ago, skaters might still need to worry about adjudicators of proper bottomwear. Insider codes of décolleté, sparkle, and roominess, modulated by elitism, racism, and anti-queer/anti-trans bias, have long differentiated classy from trashy and manly from effeminate.

With rule 7020's single subpoint (7020 A with no B), gender flexibility begins a swift explicit descent: "In pair skating competitions, only pairs of the same composition (woman and man, two women or two men) may compete against each other." Open-gender becomes binary gender and competition remains gender segregated with the addition of an m/f pair as a composite unit of uniform gender. The predominance of m/f pairs means few competition opportunities for other pairs, most prominently at the Gay Games, which occur every four years, and in occasional events within competitions called "similar pairs," understood as for fun, to the side of what skaters work hard on. The rules also identify specifically gendered roles for pairs tricks like lifts, throw jumps, and death spirals

(7100–7109). In addition, rule 7221 states that the proficiency tests "must consist of a woman and a man." Because the tests consist of a pair performing a routine to music, called a "program," with components that often require different roles of each partner, it would require time, cost, and skill mastery that would take several pages to enumerate—coaching, ice time, and more—for any pair training in a different configuration than m/f to work up two separate test routines with other partners.

What is with the difference in US Figure Skating between the openness of "two persons" and the barriers to competing in a pair other than m/f? In part you can blame the sport's top arbiter, the International Skating Union (ISU), which also regulates costume and uses the same bad math involved in policing individual athletes across sport, based on inaccurate presumptions masquerading as science that testosterone levels determine gender and athletic potential, itself conventionally gendered male. Even sports regulating gender across units greater than one use the same bad math at the core. For example, consider quadball, a sport combining rugby, dodgeball, and tag, which people play with brooms between their legs, that was recently rebranded from its name assigned at birth to distance it from the TERF creator of its fictional inspiration as a game for teen wizards. Quadball categorizes gender by gender identity and allows participants of every gender identity, thus (in theory) avoiding gender-assignment policing and the exclusion of nonbinary people. Yet its celebrated Rule Title 9¾, which stipulates that at most four of a maximum seven people on the field can share a gender identity, has the same presumption underlying binary-gender segregation: men by definition have an advantage and it's their number that must be limited (US Quadball n.d.). So, too, with pairs skating, in a sport guided overall by the perception that men are stronger and will score higher than women. Thus we have the division of singles skating into binary-gender categories, even at levels in which people competing as female routinely outscore their similarly ranked counterparts in the boy's and men's events.

We can also blame interconnected systems bigger and smaller than the ISU. Biggest: the coloniality and settler-coloniality of gender binarism and, as Maria Lugones (2010: 743) writes, the mutually reinforcing racist binarism between human and nonhuman. This is visible everywhere in sport, from the racialized measures of manhood that make Brown and Black women, especially from the global South, the primary targets of suspicion around sufficient femaleness (think also of Serena Williams) to the ascription of the ideal brain/brawn mix to white cismen, lifting them disproportionately into front offices, quarterback positions, and head-coaching slots (Karkazis and Jordan-Young 2018; Schultz 2005).

Smaller: the ISU's member organizations (the vote to change *ladies* to *women* was not unanimous) and more localized skating cultures, organizations, and individuals working to maintain norms. Or to change them. As I've discussed elsewhere and as Anna emphasizes through their podcast *The Future of Figure Skating: Conversations with Changemakers*, we are part of a growing movement to bust open the sport (Rand 2021, 2022; Kellar 2022). Skate Canada (2022a), for example, has instituted numerous changes in the past half decade. For all domestic competitions, clothing requirements are "gender neutral," with "no restrictions on skaters choosing to wear skirts, dresses, pants, or tights." In ice dance, the other two-person discipline, skaters may take qualifying tests in the (traditionally gendered) roles of lead or follow, rather than male or female. And in December 2022, the organization presented the very exciting announcement that, beginning next season (2023–24), it would introduce a change in the "Podium Pathway," which culminates in the Canadian national championship, that had already been made for "Adult" and "STAR," the two competition pathways outside the pipeline for international glory. At all levels, a pairs or dance team will consist of "two skaters," gender unregulated, with the exception of international competition, which the ISU governs" (Skate Canada 2022b, 2022c, 2022d). Importantly, these changes are part of a multifocused equity, inclusion, and accessibility project. In 2020, for example, Skate Canada changed the popular names of two turns in skating from *mohawk* and *choctaw* to *C-Step* and *S-Step*, respectively, now based on the shapes that blades make on the ice rather than on the settler-colonial mis-names of Indigenous people, apparently applied to the turns by nineteenth-century British travelers keen on US "Wild West" shows (Danyliuk 2020; *Skate Guard Blog* 2018).

USFS (2022a: 24, action 105), slow to follow, is getting somewhere, with the lead/follow protocol for testing coming next season, and more changes actively under discussion. Much at present, however, remains largely at the level of messaging, which I don't underestimate. It matters when commentators refer to competitors as "young women" instead of "young ladies." It matters that in 2022 when a Russian skating luminary trashed nonbinary Olympic pairs skater Timothy LeDuc as a freak, asking derisively what category they would compete in, USFS tweeted to "denounce hate speech" and "stand with [its] LGBTQ+ members." At the same time, that Russian luminary had a point. LeDuc and their partner, Ashley Cain-Gribble, could compete in the US National Championships and then the Olympics only because LeDuc was still registered with USFS as male. As Anna confirmed in 2022, while the USFS membership form now lists *male*, *female*, and *unspecified* on its dropdown menu for the mandatory declaration of gender, a person who picks *unspecified* (itself not the greatest category option) is locked out of all single and two-person competitions.

There's also a lot more involved than gender markers in the gendering of pairs. Gender binarism is sedimented through every aspect of training, which Anna and I come to from a telling physical disparity. Despite having a nonnormative pair of gender markers (f/f) and of gender identities (f/nb), we have an absolutely traditional height difference for pairs skating. Because I'm eight inches shorter, we can't really challenge gender norms by switching up who does what in the tricks, which our first coach had us try briefly. Anna's height makes them physically more suited to do the traditional man's role of lifter and thrower, and even to take the traditionally male role in the typical Kilian dance hold, with their arm behind my back to help steer us from behind.

Of course, people of all genders come in various sizes, so mapping height consistently onto gender requires numerous entangling, chicken-and-egg, or simply obstructionist factors to double down on gender traditionalism. Remember "Attention should be paid to the selection of an appropriate partner": organizations, coaches, parents, and others seeking to develop competitive pairs teams often put together small athletes registered as girls with larger, often older athletes registered as boys, who are sometimes adults by the time they make it to the highest levels. Cain-Gribble and LeDuc were considered gender nonconforming partly because Cain-Gribble, at 5'6", is tall for a "pair girl," to use the pairs lingo for the partner registered as female at any age or level. Physical differences, then, support ideological traditionalism. LeDuc points out that pairs often elevate "hetero-cisnormativity" choreographically, representing a "fragile girl" and a "strong man" in stories of romance or rescue (USFS 2021). That takes work to pull off in a sport that requires strength of both partners and, simultaneously, prizes the appearance of effortlessness. Put size and heteronormativity together, and you can recognize how Anna, interested in trying pairs as a child, and already tall for people gender-assigned female, never had a chance to be an "appropriate partner," even on a team without ambition or resources to aim for international glory.

The more we train—locally, regionally, and twice among and under the direction of aspiring and elite-level Canadian pairs—the more we learn, too, from doing and talking, about the devil in the details. For example, when a pair team strokes around the ice together holding hands, the skaters generally skate counterclockwise, side by side down the long axis, with the lifter to the left, perhaps a bit behind their partner (depending on who you ask), then fully behind around the corners. Do they take those positions to facilitate the switch at the corners or because the man's overall job is to feature the woman, functioning, to repeat common metaphors that sometimes still guide training, as the stem to the flower or the frame to the picture? Thus in stroking, as in holding a door, "Ladies first." Another example: Do skaters perfect the Kilian dance hold so that the boy can put the girl wherever he wants? Or so that the taller partner can help the two move safely in unison, close together, in directions they both plan to go, each working to generate speed, execute choreography, and avoid dangerous blade entanglements? The description of individual maneuvers affects the characterization of the whole pairs endeavor. We've heard all of those, sometimes from the same people, when our presence jogs them to notice that standard directions misgender Anna.

Brainstorming with them, we work to change what's hard to unembed. We also have things to figure out between us, including how we want to present ourselves as a legible, and queerly gendered, pair team. We can make a butch/femme look happen pretty easily. While a common interpretation of butch/femme as "lesbian gender" goes against our signaling goals—suggesting both "same-sex" pairing and one-masculine/one-feminine gender expression rather than gender beyond binaries—it's broadly recognizable, within and outside queer subcultures, as a queer erotic formation, made still more legible by ordinary expectations for gender contrast and romantic narrative in pairs teams. We used it for our first program to the 1980s duet "Leather and Lace," a song with lyrics that themselves blare and tweak gender contrast—the female-signaling character, in lace, being "stronger than you know" (Henley and Nicks 1981).

We also used it when we skated together within an ice dance performance ensemble, in which costume requirements limit expression altogether, and Anna and I, respectively, took the pants and skirt option. We had an indication, however, that we had queered things up in more ways than one: the choreographer's repeated comments that my pink and black hair, also too short for the "low pony [tail]" requested for aesthetic cohesion, "clashes with the costume." Besides tempering my desire to keep skating for him, that comment also well illustrates that pervasive normativity in figure skating culture, both homo- and hetero-, hands us ingredients as well as obstacles to gender queering. Not least our deviant footwear: my black skates violate the standard for people skating as female, grounded in an aesthetic ideal based on white-person skin hues that is frequently, nonetheless, still routinely forced on people of all skin tones. Anna's white skates and lifter role also don't match—no "low pony" for them either.

As we work to develop our skills and our current program—to the gender-queer Queen Latifah's version of a pairs skating classic, "I Put a Spell on You"—part of the pleasure in our skating involves thinking together and with others against traditional binary legibilities, with vocabularies enabled by costume, music, and choreography. Clare Croft (2017: 14) writes in *Queer Dance* that, from the "slide of a hand across a hipbone" to the choreography of protest in ACT UP die-ins, bodies do not merely enact transformations conceived in the mind, but are "sites to imagine, practice, cultivate, and enact social change." We're on it.

Erica Rand is professor in the Department of Art and Visual Culture and the Program in Gender and Sexuality Studies at Bates College. Her work in queer and trans sports studies includes *Red Nails Black Skates* (2012), *The Small Book of Hip Checks on Queer Gender, Race, and Writing* (2021), and ongoing participant-observation in pairs figure skating.

Acknowledgments

For help in skating and thinking pairs, thanks to: Neill Shelton, Kristin Andrews, Ann Hanson, Tina Chen, Kevin Dawes, Kirsten Moore-Towers, and Mike Marinaro; Charleen Cameron, Joe Jacobsen, and all the other coaches and skaters in the St. Margaret's Bay Skating Club pairs program; Ice Dance International, our local skating communities in Portland, Maine; and, especially Anna Kellar, the best partner and accomplice that I could imagine in the pleasure, practice, and transformation of pairs skating.

References

Bey, Marquis. 2022. *Cistem Failure: Essays on Blackness and Cisgender*. Durham, NC: Duke University Press.

Croft, Clare. 2017. Introduction to *Queer Dance: Meanings and Makings*, edited by Clare Croft, 1–34. New York: Oxford University Press.

Danyliuk, Ivan. 2020. "Why Skate Canada Renamed 'Mohawk' and Choctaw Steps?" *Skate Ukraine*, November 9. https://skateukraine.org/post/2020/terminology_change/.

Enke, Finn. 2012. "The Education of Little Cis: Cisgender and the Discipline of Opposing Bodies." In *Transfeminist Perspectives in and beyond Transgender and Gender Studies*, edited by Finn Enke, 60–77. Philadelphia: Temple University Press.

Henley, Don, and Stevie Nicks. 1981. "Leather and Lace." Written by Stevie Nicks. *Bella Donna*. Modern Records.

Karkazis, Katrina, and Rebecca M. Jordan-Young. 2018. "The Powers of Testosterone: Obscuring Race and Regional Bias in the Regulation of Women Athletes." *Feminist Formations* 30, no. 2: 1–39.

Kellar, Anna. 2022. "Introducing *The Future of Figure Skating*." *The Future of Figure Skating* (podcast), July 31. https://linktr.ee/futurefspodcast.

Lugones, María. 2010. "Towards a Decolonial Feminism. *Hypatia* 25, no. 4: 742–59.

Rand, Erica. 2021. "Skating out of the Binary." *Global Sport Matters*, July 19. https://globalsport matters.com/culture/2021/07/19/figure-skating-binary-more-inclusive/.

Rand, Erica. 2022. "At the Rink, My Feet End in Knives: An Adult Figure Skater Pivots Past Gendered, Classist, Racist Norms." *Zócalo Public Square*, February 16. https://www.zocalo publicsquare.org/2022/02/16/ice-rink-adult-figure-skating/chronicles/where-i-go/.

Schultz, Jaime. 2005. "Reading the Catsuit: Serena Williams and the Production of Blackness at the 2002 U.S. Open." *Journal of Sport and Social Issues* 29, no. 3: 338–57.

Skate Canada. 2022a. Rule 2.7, "Clothing." In *Rule Book*. Skate Canada Info Centre. https://info .skatecanada.ca/index.php/en-ca/rules-of-sport/54-competitions.html#h2-7-clothing (accessed September 17, 2022).

Skate Canada. 2022b. "Competition Program Requirements: Adult." In *Rule Book*. Skate Canada Info Centre. https://info.skatecanada.ca/index.php/en-ca/rules-of-sport/264-adult -competition-program-requirements.html#h4-1-adult-pair.

Skate Canada. 2022c. "Competition Program Requirements: Star." In *Rule Book*. Skate Canada Info Centre. https://info.skatecanada.ca/index.php/en-ca/rules-of-sport/265-star-competition -program-requirements.html#h2-pairs.

Skate Canada. 2022d. "Definition of 'Team' Updated to Reflect Gender Diversity across the Podium Pathway." Skate Canada website, December 12. https://skatecanada.ca/2022/12 /definition-of-team-updated-to-reflect-gender-diversity-across-the-podium-pathway/.

Skate Guard Blog. 2018. "How the Mohawk Got Its Name." June 8. https://skateguard1.blogspot .com/2018/06/how-mohawk-got-its-name.html.

USFS (US Figure Skating) (#usfigureskating). 2021. "A Conversation with Timothy LeDuc and Eliot Halverson." Instagram Live, June 10. https://www.instagram.com/tv/CP9HMchnhjj/ (URL defunct; accessed September 17, 2022).

USFS (US Figure Skating). 2022a. *2021–22 Combined Report of Action.* Governing Council Meeting Book. https://www.usfigureskating.org/sites/default/files/media-files/2021-22%20 Combined%20Report%20of%20Action.pdf (accessed September 17, 2022).

USFS (US Figure Skating). 2022b. *The 2022–23 Official Figure Skating Rule Book.* July. Colorado Springs, CO: US Figure Skating. https://www.usfigureskating.org/sites/default/files/media -files/2022-23%20Rulebook.pdf.

US Quadball. n.d. "Title 9¾." https://www.usquadball.org/about/title-9-34 (accessed September 17, 2022).

The MBB Manifesto
It Was Never Just Football

RAPHAEL H. MARTINS, PEDRO VIEIRA, and CARA SNYDER

Abstract The Meninos Bons de Bola (MBB, or Soccer Star Boys) is Brazil's first trans soccer team. We are a collective that welcomes transgender men, transmasculine people, trans women, and travesti players. Our manifesto recognizes that the fight for trans inclusion in athletics is part of a larger struggle against repression and fascism, and as such, we demand full access to sport for people of any and all genders and sexual orientations.
Keywords Meninos Bons de Bola, Brazil, trans, soccer/futebol, manifesto

The Portuguese version of this statement is available as online-only supplemental material at https://doi.org/10.1215/23289252-10440819 and on TSQ*Now at https:// www.tsqnow.online/.

The status of lesbian, gay, bisexual, trans, queer, intersex, asexual, and others' (LGBTQIA+) rights in Brazil is rife with contradiction; while in theory our rights are protected, in practice we face extreme levels of violence. Brazil's legislation regarding LGBTQIA+ rights is among the most advanced of any nation. For instance, same-sex marriage is legal (2011 Supreme Federal Court ruling), it is a crime to discriminate on the basis of gender or sexual orientation (2019 Supreme Court ruling), and gender affirming care is available through the Sistema Publica de Saude (Brazil's public health care system, since 2001). Yet the rates of violence against LGBTQIA+ people are also some of the worst in the world, particularly for trans and gender-nonconforming Brazilians. According to the Trans Murder Monitoring project (TGEU and Balzer n.d.), Brazil has the highest rate of trans people murdered in the world: 1,645 trans people have been killed in Brazil between January 2008 and September 2021. Taking an intersectional approach, we know that this violence disproportionately affects the members of our community who are also Black, indigenous, poor, fat, peripheral, disabled, rural, from the north or

TSQ: Transgender Studies Quarterly * Volume 10, Number 2 * May 2023   **168**
DOI 10.1215/23289252-10440819   © 2023 Duke University Press

Figure 1. A friendly match between Meninos Bons de Bola and Real Centro, June 4, 2022. The match was part of the inauguration program of the Nike multisports court in Ibirapuera Park, São Paulo. Photograph by Maurício Rodrigues Pinto, PhD student in social anthropology at the University of São Paulo and researcher at the Center for Studies on Social Markers of Difference.

northeast of the country, and immigrants. Addressing the apparent contradictions between the presence of legal rights for trans people and the absence of safety and resources for them involves putting the needs of the most marginalized at the center of struggles for justice. It is time for the LGBTQIA+ movement to center the needs and lives of trans people, and especially those of us who face multiple oppressions.

The Meninos Bons de Bola (MBB), Brazil's first trans soccer team, seeks to do this in and through *futebol* (soccer). We are a collective that welcomes transgender men, transmasculine people, trans women, and travesti players. The MBB formed in a moment of more open politics (in 2016), and we are persisting throughout the surge in right-wing movements in Brazil and around the globe. Now, at this moment, our message is perhaps more urgent than ever.

The needs of trans and marginalized people have been threatened especially since the recent rise of the Right. In Brazil, reactionaries are calling our very existence "gender ideology." They use this label to claim that the fight for our rights is a threat to the traditional family. Discrediting LGBTQIA+ and feminist struggles for justice by naming these "gender ideology" is one conservative tactic in the most recent iteration of the culture wars: a term that describes the battle for dominance of one group's practices, beliefs, and values. Part of the agenda of right-wing extremists is to keep the gender binary alive and well in areas like education, art, and sport (areas that define who we, as Brazilians, are and can be).

Figure 2. MBB team photo, São Paulo, Brazil, December 2022.
Photograph by Raphael H. Martins (@institutomeninosbonsdebolafc
on Instagram).

For instance, legislation proposed this year by representative Carlos Bolsonaro (Rio de Janeiro) seeks to prohibit trans athletes from competing.[1] This move to garner conservative political support by using trans athletes as scapegoats is unfortunately all too familiar.[2] Recognizing that the fight for trans inclusion in athletics is part of a larger struggle against repression and fascism, we demand full access to sport for people of any and all genders and sexual orientations.

Brazil's most beloved sport is soccer. We are the nation of *futebol*; since the arrival of football (as we would recognize it today) to Brazil in the late 1800s, it has been part of our national fabric.[3] And yet it is a space that has historically excluded women and LGBTQIA+ people. Women were legally banned from playing from 1940 to 1979. Today there is only one professional (cis masculine) football player who is openly queer: Richarlyson Barbosa Felisbino, who played for São Paulo Futebol Clube (1998–2021), came out as bisexual in 2022. There is one professional player who is an openly trans man, Marcelo Nascimento Leandro, who played for the Corinthians' women's team (2014–18), and who also played in the national Brazilian women's futsal team (2010, 2011, 2012). But, to this day, he seeks to play on men's teams abroad, since this has not been possible in Brazil.[4] Meanwhile, he continues to work at a travel agency. Since *futebol* in Brazil is neither open to nor prepared to welcome transgender people, we continue to demand our right to football and our right to dignity.

In advocating trans rights via the national sport, trans athletes expand both the sporting world and LGBTQIA+ movements. In 2016 in Brazil, amateur LGBTQIA+ teams began to form. The first gay cis team was Real Centro, which formed on March 6, 1990. In 2016 other cis gay teams appeared. A group of gay male cis teams—the BeesCats of Rio, the Unicornios of São Paulo, and the Futeboys of São Paulo—came together to form LiGay (2016) and held their first competition in 2017. Just two years later the league had over forty teams. We applaud any team that is challenging the cis-normative, heterosexual, and masculine norms of football. However, we have struggled to make space for trans athletes in the LiGay, which is dominated by cis gay men (who are also often wealthy and white). During our first experience competing in the LiGay's tournament in 2017 (February 11), we faced transphobic comments like, "The Little Girls' Team" and "Macho Women." Among these developments, the most surprising is that we have received more support from teams and players outside the LGBTQIA+ community, and for us that is a little sad; we would like to be welcomed and respected by our community. We are grateful for the "alternative" teams that support us, who identify as anarchist (Rosanegra, Celeste Proletária, and Havana Futebol Clube), gay (Diversus, Natus), lesbian (Boleiras Futebol Clube), and workers (O Sindicato dos Bancários). We will continue to champion trans rights in so-called LGBTQIA+ and alternative leagues, and we recognize our many allies within them. Still, our negative experiences made clear the need to create our own trans-centered spaces.

The MBB is Brazil's first trans-identified team. We began in 2016 as a team created by and for transsexual men (people designated female at birth who identify with the male gender). Our intentions (at the time) for assembling the team were to welcome trans men, to have a safe space to play *futebol*, and to have a community to exchange experiences. Trans men are particularly invisible both in the LGBTQIA+ world and in the sporting world. With the emergence of the MBB, both transmasculine men and trans-identified teams began to be seen not only in football but also in society. Over the years and with the exchange of experiences, we noticed that it was also necessary to include trans people who claimed the need to not express 100 percent of the imposed gender standards, and who do not necessarily seek to belong to this "world" of men. Today, then, the team also comprises players who are *transmasculines* (people who fit the male umbrella but do not necessarily identify as male or female), trans women (people who were designated male at birth, who identify and belong to the female gender), and *travesti* (a person who was designated male at birth, but is understood as a female figure).[5] Today there are around fifteen trans teams in Brazil and the Southern Cone (including Chile, Argentina, and Uruguay). All these teams formed after the MBB's creation, and today each team has been raising its flag for space and for the right to practice football.

The objective of the MBB is to welcome people who are trans, transsexual, and travesti to the sport of football. Our goals are to

- promote a space for meeting to facilitate a network of solidarity among peers;
- encourage sports practice;

- provide activities that enable the exchange of experiences; and
- provide enrichment through training, self-esteem, creative expression, and socialization skills.

It was never just football: our idea was always to (re)ignite the dream of playing *futebol* and to bring visibility to the bodies of trans people and travestis who are violated daily. In demanding space in football, the MBB insists that our bodies on the pitch are art, activism, and resistance.

The MBB is not about reproducing the same binaries and exclusions as sports institutions. Our group is needed to encourage others to form inclusive teams, as our rights are always being infringed. With the birth of trans teams, we can unite to show society and the world that we are capable of practicing any sport. For this to happen, professional teams need to be open to welcoming players of different genders. In addition to welcoming, they must educate their players to minimize awkwardness and eradicate transphobia. It is important that we make noise within the São Paulo Football Federation so that it changes the rules; we assert that every trans athlete must be able to join any club from the moment they manifest their passion for *futebol*. Therefore, the MBB continues in the fight to change sporting spaces that are too often prejudiced and sexist, and to bring visibility to trans football. Occupying these spaces is a political act that goes beyond football. We insist on an inclusive *futebol* for all.

Figure 3. Pedro Vieira, São Paulo, Brazil, September 2022. Photograph by Gui Christ (@guichrist onInstagram).

A Note on Process and Positionality

Rapha, Pedro, and Cara have been working together since they met at a women's soccer tournament in São Paulo in 2017 and have been close friends and collaborators ever since. As Brazil's first trans team, the MBB are trailblazers in the worlds of sport and LGBTQ+ rights, and their activism expands to encompass Afro-Brazilian and Black rights movements, antifascists, and class-based movements. In recognition of their visionary leadership, the collaborators decided to create a manifesto, using *TSQ*'s special issue on sport as motivation.

As a non-trans, white, native English-speaking, US-American academic, Cara recognizes that their relationship with the MBB requires a recognition of power differentials and a deep consideration of ethical research practices. We are always in communication to maintain a strong bond, so that we can continue to collaborate. Furthermore, we exchange experiences as well as work: Raphael and Pedro help with their research and Cara helps the Meninos with translations, planning, and applications for grants and funding.

The writing process for the MBB manifesto proceeded as follows:

Cara introduced the idea for creating and submitting a proposal for *TSQ*'s "Sports Issue," and Raphael agreed to do it, inviting Pedro to join. The timing of this issue also marks an important moment for the team—its six-year anniversary, August 26, 2022.

From there we met weekly on WhatsApp to decide and discuss what to put in the manifesto. Together we created a piece that is important to all of us. Raphael and Pedro collaborated on the history, background, and goals of the MBB, Cara contributed the structure and English translation, and we collectively edited the manifesto. We hope that the MBB manifesto will circulate widely, in both English and Portuguese.

Raphael H. Martins (ele/he) is the founder and captain of the MBB and executive director of the Meninos Bons de Bola Institute. A social educator, speaker, amateur football player, he identifies as Black and *periferico* (from the peripheries of the city). You can follow Martins and the MBB on instagram @institutomeninosbonsdebolafc.

Pedro Vieira (ele/he) is a founding member and one of the stars of the MBB. Pedro is an LGBTQIA+ rights activist and speaker in Brazil. You can follow Vieira on instagram @peduh_carll.

Cara Snyder (she/they) is assistant professor of women's, gender, and sexuality studies at the University of Louisville. Snyder has also taught at the Federal Institute of the Pernambucan Sertão and the Federal University of the São Francisco Valley in Brazil. Their research areas of interest include sport/physical cultural studies, Latin American studies, transnational feminism and LGBT studies, and digital studies. Snyder is working on a monograph that asserts women and LGBTQIA+ futebolistas in Brazil have used their visibility strategically to position themselves as protagonists in the national pastime amid the culture wars of late 1990s to today. Working with the MBB has been one of the greatest honors and pleasures of Snyder's academic career. You can find them on Twitter @1donotcara.

Notes

1. The ban would affect any competition under the jurisdiction of the city of Rio de Janeiro.
2. Other countries where debates are unfolding about bans on trans athletes include the United States, Brazil, the United Kingdom, China, and Russia.
3. We note that indigenous peoples (within the territory now referred to as Brazil) already had a sport similar to football, but that differed from the specific version brought to Brazil by the British.
4. The women's futsal world tournament was held in 2010, 2011, and 2012. In 2011 he played in the Copa America of women's futsal. For Marcelo's story in his own words, see Leandro 2020.
5. About the term *travesti*: "For a long time, the term was considered pejorative or associated with prostitution. Currently, the concept is being reclaimed and has gained political weight. There are people who proudly affirm that they are travestis due to the history of the term" (Transcendemos n.d.).

References

Leandro, Marcelo Nascimento. 2020. "Meu nome é Marcelo." *Globo*, January 28, 2020. https:// interativos.ge.globo.com/sp/futebol/materia/a-metamorfose.ghtml.

TGEU (Transgender Europe) and Carsten Balzer. n.d. "Trans Murder Monitoring." https:// transrespect.org/en/map/trans-murder-monitoring/ (accessed March 23, 2022).

Transcendemos Consultoria Em Diversidade e Inclusão. n.d. "Transcendemos explica: Principais dúvidas sobre a questão trans." https://transcendemos.com.br/transcendemosexplica /trans/ (accessed March 8, 2023).

Expanding the Repertoire of Trans Masculinities

The Cultural Legacy of Original Plumbing

EVAN VIPOND

Abstract *Original Plumbing* (*OP*) is a trans male quarterly zine cocreated and coedited by Amos Mac and Rocco Kayiatos. *OP* holds historical and cultural importance as a t4t publication made for trans men by trans men and serves as an entry point for theorizing trans masculine embodiments and subjectivities. Inspired by the format of *OP*, this piece brings together personal narrative, critical analysis, cover images, and an interview with *OP*'s cocreator and coeditor, Amos Mac.
Keywords trans masculinities, transnormativity, representation, cultural production, zine

*O*riginal Plumbing (*OP*) is a trans male[1] quarterly zine cocreated and coedited by Amos Mac and Rocco Kayiatos (also known as Katastrophe). Over the course of a decade, *OP* released a total of twenty issues, beginning with the "Bedroom Issue" (fig. 1) in fall 2009, and concluding with the "Issues Issue" (fig. 2) in winter 2019. Beyond print, *OP* sold merchandise, such as apparel and stickers, and hosted events for trans masculine communities in the United States and Canada, including launch parties for its latest issues. In May 2019 selections from each issue were compiled and published in a four-hundred-page anthology, *Original Plumbing: The Best of Ten Years of Trans Male Culture.*

    OP holds historical and cultural importance as a t4t (trans-for-trans)[2] publication made for trans men by trans men and serves as a time capsule of Anglo-American trans male culture in the 2010s. While those featured across the twenty issues of *OP* are in no way representative of the vast experiences of trans men and trans masculine people, the zine serves as an entry point for theorizing new norms of trans masculine embodiment and subjectivities, and trans male cultural production in the West. Inspired by the format of *OP*, this piece brings together personal narrative, critical analysis, cover images, and an interview with *OP*'s cofounder, Amos Mac.

TSQ: Transgender Studies Quarterly ★ Volume 10, Number 2 ★ May 2023   **175**
DOI 10.1215/23289252-10440833   © 2023 Duke University Press

The Anecdote

Back in 2009 when I was a "baby trans" completing my undergrad, my best friend and I stopped by Good for Her, a feminist and woman-owned sex shop in Toronto, for some postbreakup self-love. I was getting ready to pay for my goodies when something at the checkout caught my eye. It was the second issue of *Original Plumbing*, a new trans male quarterly zine. The cover of the "Hair Issue" features Chris E. Vargas, with his long locks, looking intently at the camera through tall, parted grass. What's this? I wondered, as I picked it up and immediately started flipping through. I was delighted to find tantalizing interviews, cultural commentary, personal anecdotes, and glossy photos featuring a variety of trans guys from across the United States, France, Germany, and even Toronto, Canada.

I was beaming with excitement. I had never come across a magazine made for and by trans guys. The lack of visibility and resources for trans masculine people left me craving the feelings of validation and sense of connection that comes with seeing oneself reflected in others. I had seen the "transvestite" and "transsexual" magazines that had been in circulation for decades, but they were predominantly for trans feminine people. I was also aware of the historically significant trans male publication *FTM Newsletter* (later *FTM International*), first published in 1987, which served as a vital resource for trans men at a time when there was a lack of visibility and few opportunities to find community. By 2009, when *OP* launched, online resources had proliferated, and people could access transition-related information more readily from the privacy of their own homes. While online communities grew, connecting trans men from around the globe, trans masculinity was vastly underrepresented and trans men remained largely invisible. As a trans male print publication, *OP* followed in the footsteps of its predecessors, but it also offered something different: a visually pleasing representation of trans masculinity and female-to-male (FTM) culture.

Each issue of *OP* is filled with thematic photo shoots, in-depth interviews, creative writing, and personal narratives, much like the teen magazines I grew up with in the 1990s. Its celebration of trans masculinity, as "beautiful, fluid, and multidimensional—complicated and provocative," was something I had not seen before (Milan 2019: ix). At the time, I had a very ambivalent relationship to the term *trans man*, identifying with the gender-neutral term *trans* instead.[3] The terms *trans masculine* and *nonbinary* were not readily available, and I felt pressure to embody, or at least embrace, hegemonic masculinity and to "fully" transition—that is, go on testosterone and have surgery—to make my gender legible to others. Notably, *original plumbing* is a term commonly used by trans men to refer to their genitals that pushes back on the cisnormative standards of male embodiment and the assumption that most trans guys pursue "lower" surgery (Mac and Kayiatos 2009: 1). Rather than trying to restrict what it means to be a trans man,

OP exemplifies that there is "no right way" to transition or embody masculinity, embracing the fluidity, complexity, and diversity of trans masculine subjectivities—from dandies, fairies, and fags, to jocks, bears, and leather daddies (Mac, see interview below). I was hooked.

Over the years, I would look forward to receiving the latest issue complete with photographs, artwork, creative writing, and illuminating interviews with trans masculine people of various shades, shapes, and sizes and from all walks of life (we're everywhere!), including artists, writers, and musicians; jocks, skaters, and stuntmen; butchers, barbers, and chefs; heroes, activists, and elders; and so many more. While it's difficult to pick favorites, my top five issues include the smutty

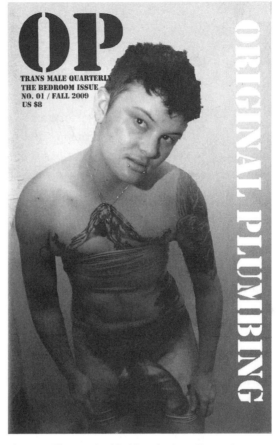

Figure 1. Photograph of Cyd Nova by Amos Mac on the cover of the "Bedroom Issue," *Original Plumbing*, no. 1, 2009.

"Bedroom Issue," the star-studded "Entertainment Issue," the inspiring "Hero Issue," the rereadable "Lit Issue," and the wonderfully creative "Art Issue." The only issue missing from my collection is the "Tattoo Issue," which sold out before I could get my hands on it. Luckily, the best parts from the issue are featured in the anthology in full-color gloss!

The Commentary

Original Plumbing, as a by-and-for trans male zine, serves as a fruitful site for theorizing trans masculinities, community formation, and cultural production (Vähäpassi 2013: 33; see also Carter, Getsy, and Salah 2014; Tourmaline, Stanley, and Burton 2017). Cultural production is often paradoxical, both reflecting and producing the subjects it represents. Through its production and circulation, *OP* (re)produces the trans male subject and trans masculine community that it seeks to reflect. Speaking to this paradox, Emmi Vähäpassi (2013: 32) explains, "[*OP*] postulates an identity, i.e., sameness, among trans men, and conveys the impression of bringing similar but separate individuals together in a kind of community based on a shared identity, while it in fact is creating this very identity." On the one hand, the trans male community *OP* claims to represent already exists; on the other hand, this community is constituted by *OP*'s contributors and readership, neither of which could predate its formation. As a young white trans masculine person exploring my identity, I came to understand myself both in relation and opposition to the representations of trans masculinity within *OP*.

OP also exemplifies the tensions between individual and collective representation and identity formations. Julian B. Carter, David J. Getsy, and Trish Salah (2014: 469) note that there is an inherent tension between "the construction and representation of *individual* trans subjects," such as the individuals represented in *OP*, and the "making and representing of trans *collectivities*," specifically the making and representation of a trans male community (see also Tourmaline, Stanley, and Burton 2017). For underrepresented communities, the representation of individuals extends beyond the subject to the collective. When *OP* was first published in 2009, there was very little public (read: cisgender) awareness of trans issues, and trans masculine representation in media and popular culture was practically nonexistent. Fast-forward ten years, and trans people are more visible than ever.[4] Despite this increasing visibility, representation of trans masculine subjects in popular culture and mainstream media is still limited, often centering the white, straight, masculine, middle-class, nondisabled trans male subject. This limited representation of trans male subjects comes to stand in for the collective, homogenizing trans masculine subjectivities by obscuring differences.

Through the lens of transnormativity, critical trans scholars have theorized how trans masculine representation in mainstream media and popular culture uphold a medical model of transition (Johnson 2016; Keegan 2013; Vipond 2015, 2021) that seeks to replicate cis male embodiment (Eckstein 2014: 27) and serves to reinforce the boundaries of the sex/gender binary (Keegan 2013; Vipond 2021). *OP* offers a counterpoint to transnormativity by demonstrating that trans men's experiences of transition and subjectivities cannot be reduced to a singular narrative or subject position. While the term *trans male* was employed throughout *OP*'s calls for writers and models, the interpretations of what it means to be trans male by *OP* readers and contributors were far more expansive than the narrow representation of trans men (e.g., white, straight, masculine) reflected in mainstream media. This expansion includes a proliferation of trans subjectivities and vocabularies—marked by a shift in terminology toward plurality (i.e., trans masculinities and femininities)—and other ways of being that reject the limits of the sex/gender binary.[5] *OP* reflects these cultural shifts by broadening the category of trans man to include trans masculine people who may not wholly identify as "male."

Original Plumbing cocreator and photographer Amos Mac recalls that he was intrigued to learn that many of the subjects of his photo shoots for *OP* "were actually more genderqueer trans masc identified, not necessarily 'FTM'" (see interview, below). Mac and his cocreator Kayiatos realized they couldn't "police" who could be included in the zine based on arbitrary standards of being trans male "enough" (interview). The transnormative discourse of being "trans enough" has been taken up by critical trans scholars (Catalano 2015; Vipond 2015; Johnson 2016; Garrison 2018; see also Spade 2003) and pushed back on by community members across various platforms, most notably Tumblr (Jacobsen, Devor, and Hodge 2021). *OP* challenges this discourse by showcasing trans masculine-of-center individuals who embody masculinity, exude femininity, or embrace androgyny, affirming trans masculinity "in all its modes and possibilities" (Milan 2019: xi). Moreover, while the earlier issues of *OP* focus more heavily on medical transition, later issues highlight other aspects of trans masculine life, including work, fashion, schooling, family, entertainment, sports, activism, politics, and arts and culture. In shifting focus away from medicalization and transition, *OP* reflects a desire by trans people to move beyond narratives of transition and celebrate all aspects of trans life.

While individual trans people may identify with or embody transnormative ideals, the privileging of a singular mode of transition and subject position results in a closed narrative that hinders the proliferation of other trans subjectivities and embodiments (Shotwell 2012: 1004; Vipond 2019: 21). Political theorist Alexis Shotwell's (2012) concept of open normativities, on the other hand, is useful for understanding how counternarratives create new possibilities that challenge the disciplinary nature of hegemonic norms. While challenging one norm may mean supplanting it with another, open normativities "prioritize flourishing and tend toward proliferation," enabling new ways of being (1003). *OP* moves away from the singularity of transnormativity toward open normativities—even as it (re)produces new norms of trans masculinity—through showcasing trans men who exist outside the narrow confines of the white, straight, masculine, middle-class subject who can be realigned within the gender binary. In doing so, *OP* offers a less cohesive but more accurate and diverse representation of trans masculine embodiments and subjectivities (Eckstein 2014: 15).

As a t4t trans male zine, *OP* resists the cisgender gaze—which too often sensationalizes, fetishizes, or pities the trans body—rejecting the impetus to make trans subjectivities and embodiments culturally intelligible to cisgender readers.[6] Enacting instead what Jack Halberstam (2005: 76) refers to as the "transgender

Figure 2. Photograph of Amos Mac and Rocco Kayiatos by Alex Schmider on the cover of the "Issues Issue," *Original Plumbing*, no. 20, 2019.

gaze," *OP* shifts the frame of cultural intelligibility away from cisgender norms and offers a more authentic (i.e., unmediated) representation of trans men that speaks back to hegemonic masculinity (Eckstein 2014: 13). This is evidenced across the various photo shoots, which "contest and complicate" cisnormative sexuality and embodiment (Pezzutto and Comella 2020: 155). Many of the photo shoots and artworks featured in *OP* depict nudity and sexual imagery, making trans masculine bodies and sexualities "knowable" (Noble 2013: 304). In doing so, trans masculine subjects take ownership over their bodies and self-expression—acts that can be "life affirming and sustaining" for both the subject and viewer (Pezzutto and Comella 2020: 155).

Representation can offer new ways of being, but it can also foreclose other possibilities and reproduce existing hierarchies, as the way "the group represents itself to itself affects what kind of trans* lives can be imagined as possible and livable lives" (Vähäpassi 2013: 33; see also Tourmaline, Stanley, and Burton 2017; Carter, Getsy, and Salah 2014).[7] While representation can "mak[e] new futures possible," it often reproduces hierarchies of in/visibility (Tourmaline, Stanley, and Burton 2017: xviii). Through erasures and omissions, certain lives—namely, Black, Indigenous, racialized, poor, or disabled—remain unimaginable within the collective imaginary (Tourmaline, Stanley, and Burton 2017: xviii; see also Carter, Getsy, and Salah 2014).

Disabled trans people, for example, are rarely represented in mainstream media or trans culture, contributing to the systemic erasure of disabled bodies. Despite the prevalence of trans persons living with disabilities,[8] there has been a failure within trans scholarship and trans communities to address ableism and issues of in/accessibility and to create the conditions for trans disabled people to thrive.[9] The limited representation of disabled trans men in *OP* reproduces these erasures and omissions.[10] At the same time, the desire to "see" disability—particularly in the context of pinup-style photographs—could contribute to the objectification and fetishization of disabled bodies and reinforce "ableist presumptions about what disability 'looks like'" (Calder-Dawe, Witten, and Carroll 2020: 132; see also Baril 2015; Baril and Trevenen 2014).[11] The underrepresentation of disabled trans people exemplifies how community formations can be emancipatory for some and exclusionary for others, most notably those who are marginalized by multiple systems of oppression (e.g., race, class, dis/ability, citizenship).

As a form of cultural production made by and for trans men, *OP* resists the cisgender gaze and the singularity of a transnormative male subject. In doing so, it contributes to the proliferation of trans male embodiments and subjectivities and expands the cultural repertoire of trans masculinities. At the same time, through omission, *OP* contributes to the ongoing erasure and underrepresentation of certain trans masculine bodies, thus demonstrating the possibilities and limitations of cultural production for individual and collective representation. With these entry points in mind, Amos Mac and I discuss *OP*'s legacy—and trans male culture more broadly, below.

The Conversation

The following interview took place over email in fall 2020.

Evan Vipond: I remember when *Original Plumbing* first launched in 2009. At the time, I didn't know of any trans male or trans masculine zines or publications. I had only come across older publications for trans women and cross-dressers. Before you and Rocco Kayiatos launched *OP*, were you aware of any FTM publications? If so, how did they inform your vision for *OP*? If not, how did the lack of publications inform your vision for *OP*?

Amos Mac: Like you, I only ever saw trans femme publications, or "cross-dresser" magazines. I found them interesting, but I couldn't relate. I really craved something that spoke to a new generation of trans guys. I didn't know any trans male publications before *Original Plumbing*, and checked magazine stands consistently for something, but never found a thing. That was exactly the drive that pushed me to create *Original Plumbing*. I've always loved magazines that are beautiful to look at. I was deeply inspired by three publications: first off, *BUTT Magazine*. What I loved about *BUTT* was the photo-heavy, artistic, great layout. *BUTT*'s audience was the artistic yet filthy homosexual, and their interviews and often nude photo shoots were with everyone from celebrities to "everyday" guys—there was something so casual and fun about the interviews. I wondered, why can't trans guys have something like that? I was also inspired by teen magazines—*Teen Beat, Bop*, and *Big Bopper*, stuff I read as a nineties kid, the kind with posters you'd tear out and tape on your bedroom wall. And lastly, I was inspired by *Physique Pictorial*, one of the first "homoerotic" publications to exist. *OP* was visually inspired by all three of those publications and was initially meant to be a one-off that I photocopied myself and sold locally. As I was photographing my friend Rocco Kayiatos for this zine idea, he pitched my idea back at me with larger ideas around how it could be ongoing, and how he could link me with trans male communities outside San Francisco where I was living at the time. This is how *OP* was launched as quarterly and became a collaborative project between Rocco and me. As far as I know from my historical research on trans publications in America, *OP* was the first trans male print magazine in the United States. Before *OP* there were of course the incredible newsletters that circulated in the 1980s and onward: *FTM International* from the United States and *Metamorphosis* from Canada. A year or so into *OP* I connected with the editor of *LAPH-FTM*, a Japanese trans male magazine that is amazing and colorful and so cool. I have some copies but can't read Japanese.

EV: I can really see the influences that *BUTT* and the other magazines you mentioned had on *OP*. As you alluded to, print (maga)zines offer something online publications don't: the tangible, physical presence of the zine can't be replicated online. At the same time, e-zines and other online platforms allow people from across the globe who would otherwise never meet to connect with one another. To me, it seems like online culture has morphed and grown rapidly over the past decade. If you were to start *OP* or another publication today, would you stick with print, or has it become passé?

AM: Because *OP* was so visual and art based (in my eyes at least), distributing it on paper was important to me, and I feel like I'd go in that direction in the future as well. When I made *Translady Fanzine* (with Zackary Drucker) it was to both collab with a trans woman and to also create accessible art that wasn't just on a screen. I still love the idea of publishing in print. I don't see myself starting an online space in the future, but I'm always happy to write for an online publication—that's fun for me.

EV: From the very first issue, *OP* did not define what it means to be trans male. This was one of the aspects of the zine that attracted me most to it. As I was still early on in my social transition, the zine offered me a community to connect with as I explored my identity as a trans masculine person by featuring a wide range of embodiments and subjectivities. This was validating and exciting to me because it made me feel like there wasn't only "one way" to be trans. Had you always envisioned the zine in this way, or did it broaden based on the contributors and readership?

AM: I knew going into *OP* that we were not there to tell anyone what a trans man was or was not, meaning we were not going to tell people some A-to-Z "way" that "made you" a trans man. Rocco and I both knew that trans male experiences were almost undefinable, and that there are as many versions of transness as there are trans people. The last thing I'd want to do is only show one version of trans masculinity in print over and over again—it was intentional to focus on how diverse trans guys are and were in terms of presentation, sexuality, personal style, relationships to their own bodies and the world around them. We've all been affected by media growing up—we've seen how TV, film, magazines (I'm speaking as a person who was a kid in the 1980s and 1990s) influence people who are coming of age. When I was a kid I saw the same type of teen on TV—straight, white, cis, able-bodied. Any other type of person was "weird" or an outcast. I didn't want *OP* to, in some small way, show our readers that there was a right or a wrong way to be *anything*.

EV: I love what you said about the expansiveness of *OP*. It both directly and indirectly spoke back to transnormativity—the medical standards of transition in which one moves wholly from one side of the binary to the other (Vipond 2015; Johnson 2016)—and the assumption that all trans men are white, straight, masculine, and physically "fit." What are your thoughts on the growing representation of trans people in mainstream media? Do you think trans representation is improving (e.g., more positive and diverse), or just more plentiful?

AM: I think it's a little bit of both, positive and plentiful, due to social media (where young people are connecting and seeing visual representations of themselves and what possibilities are out there) and trans people who are working behind the scenes and in front of the camera in TV and film who are pushing for authentic portrayals and nuanced trans storytelling (myself included). There are indeed more diverse experiences to come across when ingesting media. In books too. I just read *Cemetery Boys* by Aiden Thomas, a young adult novel, and my mind was blown. There are incredible stories being told by trans people right now, filled with nuance, and it's very exciting to me.

EV: When I first came out in the late 2000s, *nonbinary* wasn't a well-known term. I had heard of the terms *genderqueer* and the now lesser used *genderfuck*, but the connotation seemed to lean more toward gender play and fluidity rather than a static or fixed nonbinary gender identity. I found myself leaning into the label *trans guy*, as I identified with masculinity and disidentified with my assigned gender (girl). Over the last few years, *nonbinary* has gained some traction and some trans folks are coming out as nonbinary. In certain circles, this shift has resulted in a "border war" between binary/nonbinary trans identities—somewhat reminiscent of Halberstam's (1998) "Butch/FTM Border Wars."[12] Do you think there is space for binary and nonbinary identities within the trans masculine community? If *OP* were continuing today, do you imagine it would remain rooted in a more binary understanding of trans maleness, or a broader interpretation of AFAB (assigned female at birth) masculinity?

Figure 3. Photograph of Lou Sullivan, courtesy of the San Francisco GLBT Historical Society, on the cover of the "Hero Issue," *Original Plumbing*, no. 11, 2013.

AM: I believe there is room for nonbinary trans experiences within trans masculine communities. And so often we look at someone and assume they are "binary" trans male or trans female when they actually identify as nonbinary. I see that more and more online. Early on in *OP*, the language we used in casting calls asking for people to apply if interested in writing, or modeling, always included the term *trans male identified* in the magazine statement, as this was a magazine about those experiences. Then I sometimes [would] be intrigued to learn from people's mouths while I was photographing them that they were actually more genderqueer or trans masc identified, not necessarily "FTM." This was early on. Then I realized I couldn't police who should be in the magazine if they knew what the magazine was about and reached out to participate in it. Clearly they were "trans masc enough" in their own identity to connect with and want to be a part of *OP*. This goes for the people who wrote for us, too. Then in later issues we included more trans femme voices, Janet Mock and Juliana Huxtable and Kate Bornstein, while always staying true to the term *trans male culture*, because trans women were part of our culture too, and we wanted to talk about their art and amazingness.

EV: Shifting gears, which issue was the most fun or interesting to put together? Do you have a favorite issue of *OP*?

AM: I loved the "Hero Issue" with Lou Sullivan on the cover (fig. 3). The research that went into that issue, being able to dig into Sullivan's old copies of *FTM International* newsletters and learning about trans male history has inspired me so much. I still pull from that inspiration today. I have a full heart for people like Lou, Jamison Green, and Kylar Broadus, just to name a few. The work they've done and continue to do is selfless, and I feel like I'm reaping the benefits of their work and don't even realize it sometimes. They are like our grandfathers and should be honored. And the "Hero Issue" was trying to do that.

EV: What do you think *OP*'s most significant contribution has been to the trans male/trans masculine community?

AM: That's hard to answer, almost feels impossible. Perhaps a sense of community, and a visual representation of a ten-year period and a pocket of trans culture. Space.

EV: *OP* published twenty issues over the course of ten years. Why did you decide that it was time to move on? Did you feel that *OP* had run its course or that a new platform was necessary?

AM: Going into this, we knew we couldn't publish *OP* forever. It got harder to focus on the project as time went on. Our careers went in different directions. Rocco and I moved to different cities. About five years in, I was focusing full-time on television and film work to pay the bills, and that took up most of my time and creativity. The world and representation were changing on a larger level and it felt like a natural ending for us was near. We decided eventually that (issue) no. 20 would be our finale. Even after that discussion, it took a lot of time to get all twenty issues out into the world. We wanted to give *OP* a proper ending, tie up loose ends with our readers, and go out with a quiet bang. Twenty felt like the right number for that sort of thing.

Evan Vipond is a PhD candidate in gender, feminist, and women's studies at York University, in Tkaronto/Toronto, Canada. Their research explores trans rights, critical politics, and cultural representation. Vipond's work on transnormativity in popular culture appears in the anthology *TransNarratives* (2021). Their work has also been published in *a/b: Auto/Biography Studies* (2019), *Canadian Review of Social Policy* (2017), *Gender and Education* (2017), *Western Journal of Legal Studie*s (2015), and *Theory in Action* (2015). They are the cochair of the board of directors for JusticeTrans, a nongovernmental organization dedicated to access to justice for trans people in Canada.

Amos Mac is an artist and writer who explores identity, community, and "second coming of age" narratives through a queer lens. Currently a writer for the new *Gossip Girl* series on HBO Max, Mac has worked across unscripted and dramatic series, including Amazon's *Transparent*, AMC's *The Son*, and Viceland's *Gaycation*. With Aisling Chin-Yee, he cowrote *No Ordinary Man*, a documentary feature about jazz musician Billy Tipton that premiered in 2020. Mac first made waves in 2009 as the founding editor of *Original Plumbing*, the first print magazine in America to artfully document trans male culture. He published the zine for ten years.

Acknowledgments
I would like to thank Amos Mac for his openness and generosity throughout the interview. I would also like to thank Cáel Keegan, the arts and culture editor of *TSQ*, for his invaluable feedback and support during the publication process.

Notes

1.   I alternate between the terms *trans male*, *trans man*, and *trans masculine* throughout the article to highlight the proliferation of and shifts in terminology, and the diversity of trans masculine subjectivities.

2.   For a nuanced discussion of the possibilities and limitations of t4t, see Awkward-Rich and Malatino 2022.

3.   At the time, I identified as trans and used masculine pronouns (he/him). Over the years, I have come to identify with the terms *trans masculine* and *nonbinary* as well, and now use gender-neutral pronouns (*they/them*). I locate myself as a trans masculine nonbinary queer white settler who is invisibly disabled.

4.   This increased visibility has also led to hypervisibility, which can lead to heightened violence and premature death. As visibility has increased, so has anti-trans violence, which continues to threaten and claim trans lives, particularly the lives of Black trans women and trans feminine people of color. Tourmaline, Eric A. Stanley, and Johanna Burton (2017) speak to this paradox of visibility and its limitations.

5.   Another significant shift in terminology includes the use of the terms *transgender* and *trans* in favor of the older term *transsexual*, which has fallen out of favor with some trans people. Buck Angel speaks to the denigration of the term and individuals who identify as transsexual (Mac and Kayiatos 2019: 44–49).

6.   For a discussion of making trans identities culturally intelligible to cisgender readers, see Vipond 2019.

7.   Discussing the limits of visibility, Che Gossett and Juliana Huxtable (2017: 44) warn that trans visibility "doesn't challenge the hierarchical and racialized distribution of resources and/or criminalization within the regime of racial capitalism."

8.   A review of North American literature on transgender health found that 52 percent of trans people live with a disability (Davidson 2015: 43). Additional studies found that trans people experience high rates of disability, chronic illness, and mental/psychological illness (James et al. 2016: 57; Baril, Sansfaçon, and Gelly 2020: 3).

9.   The tendency to separate issues connected to transition-related medical care and gender dysphoria, and physical and mental impairment and disability emerges from the historical pathologization of trans people, ableism, and saneism within the trans movement (Baril 2015; Clare 2009, 2013, 2017; Withers 2012), and the explicit exclusion of transition-related care from disability protections (Levi and Klein 2006; Spade 2003). This is further exasperated by the centering of the nondisabled body within transgender studies, and the centering of the cisgender body within critical disability studies (Baril, Sansfaçon, and Gelly 2020; Baril and Trevenen 2014). Notably, *TSQ* has yet to publish a thematic issue on transness and disability. Articles discussing and theorizing disability have been featured, such as Jasbir K. Puar's (2014) entry titled "Disability" in the inaugural issue of *TSQ*. For scholarship that meaningfully engages with the intersections of transness and disability, see Baril 2015; Baril, Sansfaçon, and Gelly 2020; Baril and Trevenen 2014; Clare 2009, 2013, 2017; Spade 2011; and Withers 2012.

10.   Exceptions include Sanyu, a Black trans man who is chronically ill and lives with lupus (Mac and Kayiatos 2010: 16); Christopher Dowdy, a Black trans man who is visually impaired (Mac and Kayiatos 2014: 48–51); and Eli Clare, a white disabled genderqueer trans man with cerebral palsy, whose poetry is featured in issue 16 (Mac and Kayiatos 2015: 17). These examples are based on self-disclosure, meaning other contributors may also identify as disabled or live with an impairment.

11.   Many impairments are perceivable only through the presence of "visible signifiers" such as assistive technologies, mobility devices, guide dogs, and so on (Calder-Dawe, Witten, and Carroll 2020). Impairments that are not visually perceivable by others are referred to as invisible disabilities (see Baril 2015; Baril, Sansfaçon, and Gelly 2020).

12.   Zander Keig speaks to the "binary vs. non-binary divide" (Mac and Kayiatos 2019: 20).

References

Awkward-Rich, Cameron, and Hil Malatino, eds. 2022. "The t4t Issue." Special issue, *TSQ* 9, no. 1.

Baril, Alexandre. 2015. "Transness as Debility: Rethinking Intersections between Trans and Disabled Embodiments." *Feminist Review* 111, no. 1: 59–74.

Baril, Alexandre, Annie Pullen Sansfaçon, and Morgane A. Gelly. 2020. "Digging beneath the Surface: When Disability Meets Gender Identity." *Canadian Journal of Disability Studies* 9, no. 4: 1–23. https://doi.org/10.15353/cjds.v9i4.666.

Baril, Alexandre, and Kathryn Trevenen. 2014. "Exploring Ableism and the Cisnormativity in the Conceptualization of Identity and Sexuality 'Disorders.'" *Annual Review of Critical Psychology* 11: 389–416.

Calder-Dawe, Octavia, Karen Witten, and Penelope Carroll. 2020. "Being the Body in Question: Young People's Accounts of Everyday Ableism, Visibility, and Disability." *Disability and Society* 53, no. 1: 132–55.

Carter, Julian B., David J. Getsy, and Trish Salah, eds. 2014. "Trans Cultural Production." Special issue, *TSQ* 1, no. 4.

Catalano, D. Chase J. 2015. "'Trans Enough?': The Pressures Trans Men Negotiate in Higher Education." *TSQ* 2, no. 3: 411–30.

Clare, Eli. 2009. *Exile and Pride: Disability, Queerness, and Liberation.* Durham, NC: Duke University Press.

Clare, Eli. 2013. "Body Shame, Body Pride. Lessons from the Disability Rights Movement." In *The Transgender Studies Reader 2*, edited by Susan Stryker and Aren Z. Aizura, 261–65. New York: Routledge.

Clare, Eli. 2017. *Brilliant Imperfection: Grappling with Cure.* Durham, NC: Duke University Press.

Davidson, Travis W. 2015. "A Review of Transgender Health in Canada." *University of Ottawa Journal of Medicine* 5, no. 2: 40–45.

Eckstein, Ace. 2014. "Trans-Masculinities in *Original Plumbing*: Community, Queer Temporality, and Embodied Experiences." PhD diss., University of Colorado Boulder.

Garrison, Spencer. 2018. "On the Limits of 'Trans Enough': Authenticating Trans Identity Narratives." *Gender and Society* 32, no. 5: 613–37.

Gossett, Che, and Juliana Huxtable. 2017. "Existing in the World: Blackness at the Edge of Trans Visibility." In Tourmaline, Stanley, and Burton 2017: 39–55.

Halberstam, Jack. 1998. "Butch/FTM Border Wars." In *Female Masculinity*, 141–73. Durham, NC: Duke University Press.

Halberstam, Jack. 2005. *In a Queer Time and Place: Transgender Bodies, Subcultural Lives.* New York: New York University Press.

Jacobsen, Kai, Aaron Devor, and Edwin Hodge. 2021. "Who Counts as Trans? A Critical Discourse Analysis of Trans Tumblr Posts." *Journal of Communication Inquiry* 46, no. 1: 60–81.

James, S. E., J. L. Herman, S. Rankin, M. Keisling, L. Mottet, and M. Anafi. 2016. *The Report of the 2015 U.S. Transgender Survey.* Washington, DC: National Center for Transgender Equality.

Johnson, Austin H. 2016. "Transnormativity: A New Concept and Its Validation through Documentary Film about Transgender Men." *Sociological Inquiry* 86, no. 4: 465–91.

Keegan, Cael. 2013. "Moving Bodies: Sympathetic Migrations in Transgender Narrativity." *Genders*, no. 57. https://www.colorado.edu/gendersarchive1998-2013/2013/06/01/moving-bodies-sympathetic-migrations-transgender-narrativity.

Levi, Jennifer L., and Bennett H. Klein. 2006. "Pursuing Protection for Transgender People through Disability Laws." In *Transgender Rights*, edited Paisley Currah, Richard M. Juang, and Shannon Price Minter, 74–92. Minneapolis: University of Minnesota Press.

Mac, Amos, and Rocco Kayiatos, eds. 2009. *Original Plumbing*, no. 1.

Mac, Amos, and Rocco Kayiatos, eds. 2010. *Original Plumbing*, no. 5.

Mac, Amos, and Rocco Kayiatos, eds. 2014. *Original Plumbing*, no. 13.

Mac, Amos, and Rocco Kayiatos, eds. 2015. *Original Plumbing*, no. 16.

Mac, Amos, and Rocco Kayiatos, eds. 2019. *Original Plumbing*, no. 20.

Milan, Tiq. 2019. Foreword to *Original Plumbing: The Best of Ten Years of Trans Male Culture*, edited by Amos Mac and Rocco Kayiatos, viii–xi. New York: Feminist Press.

Noble, Bobby. 2013. "Knowing Dick: Penetration and the Pleasures of Feminist Porn's Trans Men." In *The Feminist Porn Book: The Politics of Producing Pleasure*, edited by Tristan Taormino, Celine Parreñas Shimizu, Constance Penley, and Mireille Miller-Young, 303–19. New York: Oxford University Press.

Pezzutto, Sophie, and Lynn Comella. 2020. "Trans Pornography: Mapping an Emerging Field." *TSQ* 7, no. 2: 152–71.

Puar, Jasbir K. 2014. "Disability." *TSQ* 1, nos. 1–2: 77–81.

Shotwell, Alexis. 2012. "Open Normativities: Gender, Disability, and Collective Political Change." *Signs* 37, no. 4: 989–1016.

Spade, Dean. 2003. "Resisting Medicine, Re/modeling Gender." *Berkeley Women's Law Journal* 18, no. 1: 15–37.

Spade, Dean. 2011. *Normal Life: Administrative Violence, Critical Trans Politics, and the Limits of the Law*. Brooklyn, NY: South End.

Tourmaline, Eric A. Stanley, and Johanna Burton, eds. 2017. *Trap Door: Trans Cultural Production and the Politics of Visibility*. Cambridge, MA: MIT Press.

Vähäpassi, Emmi. 2013. "Creating a Home in the Borderlands? Transgender Stories in the *Original Plumbing* Magazine." *QueerScope*, nos. 1–2: 30–41.

Vipond, Evan. 2015. "Resisting Transnormativity: Challenging the Medicalization and Regulation of Trans Bodies." *Theory in Action* 8, no. 2: 21–44.

Vipond, Evan. 2019. "Becoming Culturally (Un)intelligible: Exploring the Terrain of Trans Life Writing." *a/b: Auto/Biography Studies* 34, no. 1: 19–43. https://doi.org/10.1080/08989575.2019.1542813.

Vipond, Evan. 2021. "'One Hundred Percent Dude': Straightening *Degrassi*'s Adam Torres." In *TransNarratives*, edited by Kristi Carter and James Brunton, 145–64. Toronto: Canadian Scholars and Women's Press.

Withers, A. J. 2012. *Disability Politics and Theory*. Halifax: Fernwood.

Dying Ecofeminism

JEAN-THOMAS TREMBLAY

Feminism or Death
Françoise d'Eaubonne
Translated and edited by Ruth Hottell
New York: Verso Books, 2022. 352 pp.

In early 2022 Verso Books printed, under the title *Feminism or Death*, a translation by Ruth Hottell of Françoise d'Eaubonne's 1974 manifesto, *Le féminisme ou la mort*. The left-wing publisher heralded the release as a major event. D'Eaubonne is widely credited for the term *ecofeminism* and, far less credibly from Black and Indigenous vantage points, for the very politics of ecofeminism.[1] The long-awaited translation, delivered in a time of great challenges for environmentalism and feminism alike, promised ecofeminists proficient in English but not in French at once a new resource and an origin story. This narrative, like any that locates solutions to the problems of the present in a hitherto untranslated past, does not culminate in a happy or unhappy ending but peters out. No object is entirely adequate to the fantasy of recovering lost foundations.

This is what *Feminism or Death* supplies: a document, and a fascinating one at that, of movement politics in the third quarter of the twentieth century. In the years leading up to the book's original publication, d'Eaubonne had joined and left the Parti communiste français (French Communist Party), cofounded the Front homosexuel d'action révolutionnaire (Homosexual Front for Revolutionary Action), and signed the Manifeste des 343 (Manifesto of the 343) declaring that she had had an abortion. These commitments and others—to working through feminism's collusion with the oppression of sex workers, to facilitating exchanges with the radical arm of the US women's movement—collide in *Feminism or Death*. The result embraces, in content and form, the dynamics of coalition building. We are far from Shulamith Firestone's (1970) *The Dialectic of Sex*, to which d'Eaubonne is nevertheless often sympathetic. Firestone's dedication to internal consistency in a book that presents itself as a prequel to Karl Marx and Friedrich Engels's materialism matches Andrea Long Chu's (2019: 18) formulation of ethics as a "commitment to the bit." D'Eaubonne's writing, by contrast, evokes the rowdiness of organizing. It is in turn thrilling, confusing, distracting, and boring—like a meeting.

This is what *Feminism or Death* does not supply: much insight on environments or ecologies. D'Eaubonne operates neither on the environmental scale (the surrounding conditions of organic life) nor on the ecological scale (the relationship between organisms and their environments) but on a planetary scale that we have come to associate with climate rhetoric (Chakrabarty 2020). Rather late in *Feminism or Death*, d'Eaubonne names overpopulation and resource exhaustion as the "two most immediate threats of death today" (194) or, in the trendy parlance of risk management unpacked by Joshua Schuster and Derek Woods (2021), the greatest sources of existential risk. These threats are products of a five-millennia-old "phallocratism" (99) that d'Eaubonne condenses as "the male system—the system as male (and not capitalist or socialist)" (194). Women's reproductive capacity, in her assessment, delineates the terrain on which the struggle for planetary survival ought to play out. D'Eaubonne describes "the only mutation that can save the world" as follows: "Not a 'matriarchy,' of course, or 'power to women,' but the destruction of power by women, and finally, the way out of the tunnel: egalitarian administration of a world reborn (and no longer 'protected' as the soft, first-wave ecologists believed)" (195). Rather than investigating milieux and ecosystems, d'Eaubonne equates womb and planet to promote antinatalism as a buffer against extinction.

From one angle, d'Eaubonne's antinatalism may be said to refute a worrisome variety of ecofeminism currently in circulation. This variety mobilizes a conservationist doctrine to "gender-critical" ends. *Guardian* lead writer Susanna Rustin (2021), for instance, appeals to resource conservation to describe medical transition as an act against nature. Medical transition thereby signals a hubristic disregard for the fact that "human bodies have limits," which she compares to "the failure to address the implications of our planet's finite resources." Rustin's case isn't an isolated one. We cannot overstate the readiness with which climate activists, as well as scholars of environments and ecologies, currently traffic in such ecofeminist-lite prohibitions against the arrogance of disturbing the so-called natural course or order of things. This traffic makes environmental politics and studies often complicit with antitransness, leaving their adherents with a depleted notion of what it means to be a subject of biological transformation and variation.

A defense like Rustin's of the integrity of the body assigned female *or* male is necessarily eugenicist. Rustin does not reject medical activities wholesale, only, it seems, those that detach medicine from the optimization of reproductive capacity. It is difficult, then, to grasp Rustin's fidelity to "limits" as anything other than mandated reproduction. The sadistic imposition of this mandate by trans-exclusionary radical feminists (TERFs) marks a late stage in the British colonial and imperial enterprise. In an empire not dying but zombified, as Sophie Lewis (2019) and Jules Gill-Peterson (2021) have suggested in their public writing, gender nonconformity, especially among children, grants primarily white British women an alibi for repeating the colonial pleasures of controlling racial others deemed too unruly to observe the limits of their own bodies.

D'Eaubonne's reluctance to make the child the horizon of political intelligibility feels refreshing in a context in which both environmentalists and TERFs have fulfilled Lee Edelman's (2004) worst nightmares by declining to elect other subjects worthy of protection. And yet d'Eaubonne never evades eugenics, her dream of population reduction recalling many an anti-Black and ableist discourse. Whether she even desires an evasion is unclear. *Feminism or Death* makes extensive detours to socio-zoological experiments about rat demography and (more critically, at least) the Nazi death camps. The manifesto does not make a strong case against eugenics, only one against the eugenics inconducive to her vision of rebirth.

This reading of *Feminism or Death* may interfere with certain colonial and antitrans discourses, but the manifesto is not, by any stretch of the imagination, anticolonial or trans affirming. Anxieties around that fact are palpable across the prefatory materials included in the Verso volume. In their newly translated introduction to the 2021 edition of *Le féminisme ou la mort*, ecofeminist scholars Myriam Bahaffou and Julie Gorecki vow to "state things plainly" by declaring d'Eaubonne's manifesto "problematic in that it ignores one fundamental fact: colonization" (xxvii). The assertion prevents accusations of complicity but misses the point. Colonization is not absent from *Feminism or Death*. It is everywhere, negated.

Negation at times looks like d'Eaubonne's insistence that existential peril is a product not of capitalism—an analysis of which would require an account of colonialism and imperialism—but of phallocratism. Most often, d'Eaubonne negates the fact of colonization by confining it to analogies. She once muses that women have to define themselves in relation to men, "the same as I, as a goy, have to define myself in relation to anti-semitism, and as a Western woman in relation to the Third World" (28–29). Elsewhere, she ponders, "In the past, 'sex' signified 'woman.' Sex and woman constituted the hidden face of the earth. The black continent" (161). The "Third World" and the "black continent" are, themselves, colonial and imperial figures. In the first excerpt, the Third World, which by occupying the same position as men and anti-Semitism gets coded as a threat, exists only as a referent for the Western woman to define herself against. In the second excerpt, sex or woman is likened to the black continent, but here also the referent is negated. For the metaphor to work as one, readers must grasp that sex or woman is not, in fact, the black continent. No sooner is racial and cultural difference invoked than it is discarded. *Feminism or Death* does not create a gap that anticolonial thought would get to fill. Instead, it exemplifies a tendency to treat Black or Indigenous life as illustrative of whiteness, rather than itself.

Anxieties around antitransness, for their part, show up in a new foreword by ecofeminist philosopher and historian of science Carolyn Merchant. Whereas Bahaffou and Gorecki volunteer a lacuna in the manifesto, Merchant is willing to consider the problem of essentialism—whether "women (and men) have innate, unchanging characteristics (or essences)" (xiii)—only abstractly, as it pertains to ecofeminism on the whole. Not a word on how essentialism informs d'Eaubonne's thinking in particular. Merchant notes that, "in recent years, new questions have arisen about the relationships between trans feminism and ecofeminism" (xiv). The comment both overstates the recency of said questions and downplays the well-documented fact of antitransness in ecofeminist circles. Already in 1978, Mary Daly ([1978] 1990), an obvious precursor of Rustin, had published her remarks on the "Frankenstein phenomenon" (69), or the "necrophiliac," "insane desire for power, the madness of boundary violation" (70–71). This framing of transness would have a sufficient impact on feminist, gay, and lesbian thought and action for historian Susan Stryker (1994) to see fit to address it in her article "My Words to Victor Frankenstein above the Village of Chamounix," widely considered key to the emergence of trans studies.

Loath to implicate d'Eaubonne in ecofeminism's antitransness, or even to mention *Feminism or Death*'s undeniably narrow notion of anatomy and gestation, Merchant gestures vaguely:

> Transgender and transsexual people have equal rights within the larger struggle for human rights and in actions on behalf of the environment. Transgender individuals have the same entitlements to health care, legal rights, and institutional privileges as do cisgender women and men. They may argue that nature itself is not a woman or a mother but, if personified, could be termed "they" or nongendered. One's relationship to nature could be personal, open, embracing, and caring, as well as scientific, ecological, and non-domineering. Cisgender men, cisgender women, and transgender persons would all participate equally in ecofeminist and humanist actions, policies, and philosophies to save the environment. (vix)

Merchant's prose brings to mind the sanitized calls for kindness we would expect from official communication cleared by a legal team. Some of her claims are plainly false: in many locations, trans people do not "have equal rights" or "have the same entitlements" to services and privileges. The resolution she rushes—that "if both women and men, as ecofeminists, care for and take care of nature, then nature can survive well into the future" (xiii)—reads as a non sequitur. Merchant contributes liberal wishful thinking about broadening the terms of participation in ecofeminism.

It does not bode well for d'Eaubonne's posthumous Anglophone career that those tasked with ushering her manifesto into the twenty-first century would rather foreground what they believe it lacks, or even look away, than evaluate its content. Why this timidity? Is the white, Western ecofeminism typified by *Feminism or Death* irremediably toxic?

Perhaps. It certainly would have been easier to reply in the negative a few years ago, prior to the increased platforming of antitransness. Fueled and funded by right-wing Christian interests, the current wave of antitransness is nevertheless legitimated by pundits whose pick-and-choose approach to ecofeminist principles has sought to protect one kind of nature—a fantasy of binary sex—above others. If Rustin's op-ed and the wave of antitrans concern that shares its rationale are indicative of ecofeminism's leap into the mainstream, we are forced to admit that the movement or ideology has not brought us any closer to gender and sexual liberation or to a revolutionary transition out of environmentally damaging systems. That by squinting we might see in d'Eaubonne's antinatalism alternatives to the maternal and child fetishes does not mean that *Feminism or Death* holds the key to a white, Western ecofeminist trajectory that radically deviates from our antitrans and colonial present. It may be time to reject the terms by which we have been implored by d'Eaubonne and her champions to choose between ecofeminism and death.

Jean-Thomas Tremblay is assistant professor in York University's Humanities Department. Tremblay is author of *Breathing Aesthetics* (2022) and, with Andrew Strombeck, coeditor of *Avant-Gardes in Crisis: Art and Politics in the Long 1970s* (2021). Current book projects include "The Art of Environmental Inaction" and, with Steven Swarbrick, "Negative Life: The Cinema of Extinction."

Note

1. An open letter by Audre Lorde (1979) decrying Mary Daly's "dismiss[al of] our Black foremothers" tallies early evidence of white ecofeminism's foundational negation and absorption of Black and Indigenous experiences, mythologies, and cosmologies.

References

Chakrabarty, Dipesh. 2020. *The Climate of History in a Planetary Age.* Chicago: University of Chicago Press.

Chu, Andrea Long. 2019. *Females: A Concern.* New York: Verso.

Daly, Mary. (1978) 1990. *Gyn/Ecology: The Metaethics of Radical Feminism*. New York: Beacon.

Edelman, Lee. 2004. *No Future: Queer Theory and the Death Drive*. Durham, NC: Duke University Press.

Firestone, Shulamith. 1970. *The Dialectic of Sex: The Case for Feminist Revolution*. New York: Bantam.

Gill-Peterson, Jules. 2021. "Gay for History." *Sad Brown Girl*, July 21. https://sadbrowngirl.substack .com/p/gay-for-history.

Lewis, Sophie. 2019. "How British Feminism Became Anti-trans." *New York Times*, February 7. https://www.nytimes.com/2019/02/07/opinion/terf-trans-women-britain.html.

Lorde, Audre. 1979. "An Open Letter to Mary Daly." History Is a Weapon. https://www.history isaweapon.com/defcon1/lordeopenlettertomarydaly.html.

Rustin, Susanna. 2021. "My Hope for a More Open Discussion of Women's and Trans Rights Is Fading." *Guardian*, October 13. https://www.theguardian.com/commentisfree/2021/oct /13/discussion-women-trans-rights-feminists.

Schuster, Joshua, and Derek Woods. 2021. *Calamity Theory: Three Critiques of Existential Risk*. Minneapolis: University of Minnesota Press.

Stryker, Susan. 1994. "My Words to Victor Frankenstein above the Village of Chamounix: Performing Transgender Rage." *GLQ* 1, no. 3: 237–54.

Recovering Doubt and Uncertainty as a Means of Teaching and Learning

KONSTANTINOS ARGYRIOU

El feminismo queer es para todo el mundo
Gracia Trujillo
Madrid: Catarata, 2022. 126 pp.

Where is queer theory situated within the current Spanish framework? Faced with recent reactionary turmoil and aggressiveness that have rampaged in the LGBTQI+ community in Spain during the last few years, amid the COVID-19 pandemic, Gracia Trujillo offers an indispensable, restorative essay that reintroduces queer terminology and history under a new guise. Queer is discussed as a resistance against the heteronormative sociocultural regime, but also as a boundary crossing. Drawing heavily on bell hooks's work, the book also raises the possibility of inhabiting the limits of intelligibility. Difference is portrayed as a space of encounter, instead of a separating mark.

Queer, in this sense, is also a leakage, a barrier to definition. The author embraces this ambiguity since the very first chapter, by detaching the notion from identity politics and reassembling it as a street movement based on affect, provisionality, and strategic deidentification. The reappropriation of the slur—as an escape route from the preestablished sex-generic system, a peripheral place of enunciation of sexuality, a critique of the naturalization of sex, a micropolitics of traversing or becoming, and a "space of reception and not of division between struggles" (Trujillo 2022: 27)—has been key in deconstructing the prevailing privatized gay culture. The increasing semantic inclusiveness/umbrella use of *queer* needs to assume the conflicts between Anglo-Saxon terminological impositions and preexisting or alternative categorizations.

TSQ: Transgender Studies Quarterly ★ Volume 10, Number 2 ★ May 2023 **195**
DOI 10.1215/23289252-10440861 © 2023 Duke University Press

The second chapter emphasizes historical political tensions between the 1970s and the 1990s. ACT UP mobilizations, together with the questioning of the liberal agendas of achieving "same-sex" marriage, demonstrate how the nascent queer movement was rooted in strategic Spivakian essentialism, extremely critical of the prevailing identity politics of that time. Identities, within the queer prism, would be read as spontaneous, neither given nor merely acquired, but ephemeral and highly contextualized encounters, which are opposed to the idea that, in order to claim rights, prior subjectivation is required. Teresa de Lauretis ended up discouraged by the emptying of the revolutionary meaning of queerness and the perpetuation of silences by institutionalized LGBT discourses.

The third chapter reveals how many key figures in queer theory have been women—despite the misrepresentation by certain current discourses, which use *queer* as a euphemism for *gay agenda*. Particularly after the 1980s, the plural signifier *women* is political rather than biological. The hybridization of the universal subject has assumed various forms according to the corresponding conceptualizations, moving through Monique Wittig's lesbian(-no-woman), Gloria Anzaldúa's mestiza, Donna Haraway's cyborg, or Rosi Braidotti's nomadic subject, among others. This chain of terms, proposed to resignify the standard way of conceiving women as monolithic subjects, has served to mobilize discourses from the margins, from peripheral places of enunciation. Trujillo grasps the opportunity to criticize the inopportune drifts of Simone de Beauvoir's reflections, with exclusionary or, paradoxically, naturalizing purposes.

Subsequently, Trujillo discusses the abuse of power by a certain radical feminist sector, particularly institutional, that has incited separatism to ensure its privileged position: "Currently, the 'radfem' sector has appropriated the label of 'radical' feminism, even misrepresenting the contributions of this approach to justify the exclusion of trans* women from the feminist movement. We must dispute that label: radical feminism has a very powerful genealogy that is also ours" (2022: 63; translation my own). Deliberately or perhaps out of ignorance, this reactionary radfem sector seems to forget or underestimate that the Dangerousness Law of the late Francoist regime aimed to "normalize" lesbian women, who were expelled from asylums and convents, and who frequently underwent conversion therapy. The presumed dangerousness of the lesbian body seems to have shifted, currently, toward a series of dissident bodies, such as those of racialized, migrant, and trans women, who are criminalized precisely for not obeying the normative schemes of "being a woman." Hostility, both social and legal, risks the amnesia of subordinate and precarious genealogies, which have not achieved securing their testimonial authority to this day.

Chapters 5 and 6 defend protest and grassroots activism as motors of the queer movement—Trujillo's own inspiring trajectory attests to her assertions. The recent far-right and radfem backlash, alongside the epidemiological restrictions that reduced open public dialogue, paved the way for hate speech to grow disproportionately. Contemporary Spanish sex wars make no mistake in perceiving the connectedness of queer claims; on the contrary, they benefit from this realization, by turning disadvantaged social groups against each other, as well as by dividing issues that should better be understood conjointly (for instance, sex work and trans inclusion).

The last chapter, perhaps the most revolutionary contribution of the book, details a queer pedagogy that serves to reconnect body and mind. Since heteropatriarchy is a political regime that feeds on closets, the school becomes its deviation surveillance device. Transgressive pedagogies destabilize this oppressive hegemony, not through monolithic inclusion of diversity in education but, rather, through intersectional claims that question the linear, desexualized knowledge production which avows cisheterosexuality as a given.

Overall, this book offers situated insights that are of great analytical and political value during this crucial contemporary moment that queer activism and scholarship are facing in Spain. The educational capacity and semantic cohesion of the text deserve an honorable mention.

Konstantinos Argyriou (he/him) is a PhD candidate in interdisciplinary gender studies at the Institute of Philosophy of the Spanish National Research Council and the Autonomous University of Madrid. His research focuses on trans people's and psychologists' attitudes toward mental health services.

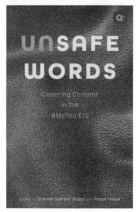

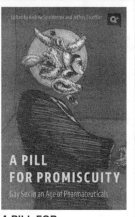

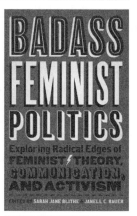